I0035363

Top Market Strategy

Top Market Strategy

Applying the 80/20 Rule

Dr. Elizabeth Rush Kruger

business**expert**
Press

Top Market Strategy: Applying the 80/20 Rule
Copyright © July 2008, July 2010, Strategic Power®
May 2011, Business Expert Press, LLC

All Rights Reserved. No part of this publication may be reproduced
in any form or by any means without first obtaining the specific writ-
ten permission from Dr. Elizabeth Rush Kruger. You are restricted from
photocopying or using any mechanical or electronic means to reproduce,
transmit, or store any part of this document in a retrieval system without
her permission.

ISBN-13: 978-160649-310-6 (paperback)

ISBN-13: 978-160649-311-3 (e-book)

DOI 10.4128/9781606493113

A publication in the Business Expert Press Marketing Strategy collection

Collection ISSN: 2150-9654 (print)
Collection ISSN: 2150-9662 (electronic)

Cover design by Jonathan Pennell
Interior design by Scribe, Inc.

First edition: August 2011

10 9 8 7 6 5 4 3 2 1

Printed in the United States of America.

Strategic Power® is a registered trademark of Strategic Power

Abstract

Research verifies that the 80/20 rule summarizes the stable relationship of inputs to outputs—including the impact of customers on the profit of a business. According to this universal law, a business can predict that the most profitable 20% of its customers generates 80% of its profit from customers and that customers in this top market segment are 16 times more profitable than customers in the bottom market segment. Thus when a business replaces all customers in the bottom market segment with new customers in the top market segment, the business can expect to quadruple its profit from customers.

Virtually any business can achieve this amazing outcome by fully implementing the three steps of a top market strategy:

1. Segment customers by their profitability, and distinguish the most profitable 20% of customers.
2. Select this top market segment as the target market, and focus resources on these loyal, heavy users.
3. Execute research-driven marketing strategies to attract and retain customers in this target market.

This book reveals insider secrets for business success by demonstrating how to dramatically multiply profit from customers:

- Part I reviews the fundamentals of marketing and survey research.
- Part II describes the 80/20 rule and its previous applications.
- Part III applies the 80/20 rule to profit from customers.
- Part IV illustrates each of these steps with a practical case example.
- The Appendices document how to accomplish these steps using Microsoft Excel software.

This new application of the 80/20 rule empowers managers and marketers to attract and retain highly profitable customers, thereby quadrupling their profit from customers.

Keywords

Management, marketing, business plan, marketing plan, marketing strategy, strategic planning, strategic marketing, Pareto's 80/20 rule

Contents

Illustrations

Figures

Photos

Charts

Icons

Key point

Insider Secret

Conclusion

Tables

Foreword

Top Market Strategy: Applying the 80/20 Rule is a valuable tool for entrepreneurs and business managers who need a practical way to improve profit by replicating their best customers. I speak from my experiences as a regional manager for a large national organization and as an entrepreneur. Throughout my years of selling and servicing insurance, the results were exactly as Dr. Kruger predicts in her book. In both the large and small businesses, 80% of our revenue and business profit came from the top 20% of our customers.

As a result, we decided to personally service the top 20% of our customers and to automate services with the bottom 80% of our customers. Since our sales force now services only the top 20% of their previous book of customers, we increased their sales commission from 20% to 25% to maintain their earning levels—and to motivate them to acquire highly profitable new customers. According to the 80/20 rule, we expect these new customers to be 16 times more profitable than their previous customers.

Before reading this book, I justified our stratified service approach with the 80/20 rule, but now I realize that this relationship between inputs and outputs is a universal law. What Dr. Kruger has done for any business is to lay out a detailed, ready-to-use process for growing highly profitable customers. This process starts by using simple statistical tools to understand the most profitable 20% of your customers. Then Dr. Kruger goes on to explain how to focus your marketing strategies on fulfilling their wants and needs and to grow more customers just like them.

Robert Iocco, CPA, CIC
President, Trust Point Insurance
Bristol, Virginia

Preface

The 80/20 rule summarizes a universal law that predicts the relationship of inputs to outputs—and even governs the impact of customers on your business profit. According to this law, you can expect that the top 20% of your customers will generate 80% of your profit from customers and be 16 times more profitable than your other customers. *Top Market Strategy: Applying the 80/20 Rule* demonstrates the three steps to apply this universal law in your business:

1. Segment your customers by their profitability and distinguish the most profitable 20% of your customers.
2. Select this market segment as your target market.
3. Focus your strategic marketing plan on serving this target market.

This book reveals insider secrets for your business success, explains that a top market strategy can dramatically multiply your profit from customers, and demonstrates with a practical example how to implement this process in any business—even yours. You will learn to do the following:

- Probe for insights, create a survey, sample your customers, and obtain valid responses.
- Use statistics in Microsoft Excel to distinguish customers in your top market segment from other customers.
- Create effective marketing strategies for attracting highly profitable new customers to your business.

This universal law predicts that your profit from customers will quadruple when your marketing strategies serve your most profitable customers.

PART I

Marketing Fundamentals

CHAPTER 1

Essentials of Marketing

1.1 Marketing

Simply stated, *marketing* facilitates the exchange of value between parties. This means that your customers are willing to pay a higher price when your business offers more value. Thus your *profit from customers* measures how well your business responds to the desires of its customers, thereby fulfilling the golden rule:

"Do unto others as you would have them do unto you."[1]

A business can market anything—a product, service, location, candidate, or issue—by making decisions relative to four basic tools: product, price, place, and promotion (Table 1).

Table 1. Tools of the Marketing Mix

Tools	Aspects
Product	Brand name, design, benefits, features, quality, packaging, labeling, warranty, add-on services, and line extensions
Price	Retail price, leasing, payment plan, interest rate, credit policies, price discounting, trade-ins, free services, and bundling with other items
Place	Length and members of the distribution channel; governance; agreements; sales training; technical training; commissions; bonuses; territories; warehousing; logistics; transportation; delivery; on-site promotion; customizing; and policies on sales, collections, and returns
Promotion	Reputation, unique selling proposition (USP), graphics, heading, copy, media vehicles, timing, advertising, sales promotion, buzz, viral marketing, direct marketing, Internet marketing, personal selling, referrals, sponsoring, and publicity

---

This chapter is based on Kotler and Armstrong (2010).

1.2 Marketing Strategy

🔑 **Every successful business implements a strategic marketing plan that distinguishes the business from its competitors.**

A strategic marketing plan specifies how a business will serve its target market through its product, pricing, distribution, and promotional strategies. The three steps in developing a strategic marketing plan are segmenting customers, targeting a market segment, and positioning the business:

1. *Segmenting* divides (i.e., segments) a market into subgroups (i.e., market segments) and describes the distinguishing characteristics and desires of each market segment.
2. *Targeting* evaluates various market segments, selects the best one as the target market, and focuses resources on this market segment.
3. *Positioning* differentiates a business from its competitors by implementing distinctive marketing strategies for serving its target market.

🔑 **A business maximizes its profit by segmenting the market, targeting its most profitable market segment, and positioning the business to serve this target market.**

1.3 Market Segmentation

The *market* of a business consists of all who have the desire, authority, and ability to buy from the business, either now or in the future. *Market segmentation* divides the market into distinct market segments and describes their distinguishing characteristics. Members of a market segment are *homogeneous* (i.e., similar) to one another, yet *heterogeneous* (i.e., distinct) relative to other market segments. Market segmentation can divide customers into market segments by their demographic, geographic, psychographic, or behavioral characteristics (Table 2).

👤 **Behavioral segmentation is more direct and actionable than other approaches to segmentation since this process categorizes customers by their buying behavior.**

Table 2. Bases for Segmentation

Categories, sources, and costs	Bases for segmentation
Demographic segmentation Source is government Low cost	Gender, age, income, occupation, socioeconomic status, education, size of the family, stage of the family life cycle, religious affiliation, ethnicity, language, and nationality
Geographic segmentation Source is government Low cost	Climate, population density, trade agreements, time zone, region, nation, district, state, county, market area, city, ZIP code, and census tract
Psychographic segmentation Source is subscriptions and memberships Medium cost	Personality, lifestyle, attitudes, social class, and values
Behavioral segmentation Source is customers High cost	Occasion, evaluation, readiness, user status, end use, benefits sought, usage rate, problem, desire, media preference, loyalty, and profitability

1.4 Target Marketing

Target marketing is the process of evaluating market segments and selecting the best one as the target market. Marketers evaluate each market segment relative to certain criteria (Table 3) and multiply these scores to calculate each market segment's overall score as a predictor of its long-term profitability. Since scoring low on any criterion dramatically lowers its overall score, one "fatal flaw" can disqualify a market segment from selection as a target market.

> A market segment must score well on each criterion to be selected as a target market.

1.5 Strategic Positioning

Marketing strategies should respond to the distinctive characteristics and desires of its target market. *Strategic positioning* differentiates a business from its competitors by uniquely serving its target market.

> A strategic marketing plan should position a business so that its target market perceives that the business serves them and them alone.

Table 3. Criteria for the Target Market

Criteria	Requirements
Identifiable	Members of the market segment are similar to one another yet are significantly different from other customers.
Actionable	The business can differ from its competitors by responding to the unique motivations and desires of the market segment.
Underserved	The business can fulfill an unsatisfied desire of the market segment.
Accessible	The business can target the market segment with promotions and publicity
Substantial	The business expects high profit due to the market segment's size, high usage rate, or insensitivity to price.
Growing	The business expects that economic, demographic, cultural, governmental, environmental, or technical trends will increase the demand of the market segment.
Sustainable	The business can generate a long-lasting competitive advantage with the market segment through capital investment, expertise, legal protection, or economies of scale.

Coordinating your product, pricing, distribution, and promotional strategies sends a cohesive message to your target market, thereby increasing your profit. However, mixed messages tend to decrease your profit.

A business maximizes its profit from customers when its marketing strategies focus on serving its target market.

1.6 Research Phases

The characteristics of current customers best predict the characteristics of potential customers.

Market segmentation guides marketers to select the best target market and to create marketing strategies that distinctly position the business as serving this market segment. This process has three phases:

1. *Exploratory research* elicits response options for closed-ended survey questions.

2. *Survey research* quantifies responses from a proportionally representative sample of current customers.
3. *Segmentation research* categorizes respondents into market segments
and describes the distinctive characteristics of each market segment.

CHAPTER 2

Decisions About Customer Surveys

2.1 Exploratory Research

Usually researchers gain insights for a customer survey by conducting in-depth interviews with a few diverse customers until their answers become repetitive (Chapter 8). Their open-ended probing reveals the respondents' thoughts, feelings, motivations, perceptions, and other qualities. Then researchers summarize each respondent's answers, aggregate these profiles into a summary table, and select common answers as response options for survey questions.

> Use open-ended questions in exploratory research so you can avoid them in survey research, thereby lowering your cost for coding and improving your response rate.

2.2 Sampling

The *population* for a customer survey is all customers who qualify for the survey, whereas a *sample* is a group of customers selected from the population. *Probability sampling* methods assume that the entire sample responds—an unrealistic requirement—so most survey researchers prefer *nonprobability sampling* in general and *quota sampling* in particular (Table 4). They usually perceive quota sampling to be less biased and more cost effective than other sampling methods.

> When a quota sample is sizeable and proportionally represents all potential respondents, you can expect that the responses of these respondents generalize to the population.

This chapter is based on Churchill and Brown (2007).

Table 4. Nonprobability Sampling

Methods	Descriptions	Uses	Evaluations of sampling error
Convenience sampling	Select the most convenient people.	To obtain quick or cheap survey research	Highly biased sample
Judgment sampling	Select experts on the topic of the research.	To evaluate concepts and forecast trends	Possibly a biased sample
Snowball sampling	Ask respondents to recommend others.	To overcome a low incidence rate	Unrepresentative sample
Quota sampling	Select respondents who fulfill quota requirements.	For most survey research	Assumed to be a proportionally representative sample

2.3 Sample Size

Experience teaches us that the responses of a large sample tend to balance out and better represent the population of all potential respondents, whereas the responses of a small sample (i.e., less than 30 respondents) tend to skew. Thus we can only analyze a subgroup of a sample if we expect at least 30 reponses. For example, when 150 unbiased respondents answer a question with 5 possible answers, we expect 30 responses for each response option.

We can predict the population's responses when we analyze at least 30 responses from a proportionally representative sample.

2.4 Validity and Reliability

Validity refers to the relevance of the data, whereas *reliability* refers to the accuracy of the data. If the data are not relevant, why worry about their accuracy? Compared to a larger sample, a small sample has less accurate responses due to random sampling error, but validity errors are more dangerous than inaccuracy (Table 5).

To minimize total error, first make sure the data will be valid, and then use any remaining money to increase the size of your sample.

Table 5. Validity Errors

Types of error	Definitions	Examples
Population error	The definition of the population is vague.	Researcher tests the taste of a new dog food by surveying dog owners, rather than dogs.
Frame error	The contact list is biased.	Interviewer calls from a telephone directory that leaves out students, low-income households, unlisted people, and those without a landline.
Sampling error	The respondents are not representative.	A waitress asks high-tipping customers to evaluate her service, but skips her other customers.
Nonresponse error	The respondents differ from nonrespondents.	Respondents report problems, but satisfied customers do not respond to the survey.
Interviewer error	Respondents are unable or unwilling to answer so they skip a question.	Respondents are unable to remember past events (e.g., "What did you eat yesterday?"), or they are unwilling to answer embarrassing questions (e.g., "Have you stopped beating your wife yet?")

2.5 Levels of Data

A question defines a *variable*, while an answer to a question defines a *value*.

Researchers quantify answers to closed-ended questions by assigning a code number to each response (i.e., value). Metric responses can be summarized in many ways, but nonmetric responses can only be summarized by frequency counts and percentages. A question elicits *nonmetric* values when respondents select a quality from mutually exclusive response options:

1. Nonmetric questions with categorical response options elicit *nominal* values (i.e., names). The standard practice is to report the

percentages of nominal responses in descending order, such as "The customers are 51% female and 49% male."

2. Nonmetric questions with sequential response options elicit *ordinal* values (i.e., ranks). It is best to report the percentages of ordinal responses in their natural order, such as "Over half (55%) of the customers are under 49 years old, but many (45%) are at least 50 years old."

🔑 **Nonmetric values such as *age category* cannot be averaged, whereas metric values such as *years of age* can be averaged.**

A question elicits *metric* values when respondents answer with a quantity:

1. Metric questions that are answered with an equal-interval rating scale elicit *interval* values (i.e., ratings). Usually researchers report the average ratings in descending order, such as "On a 5-point Likert rating scale, my personality is competitive (2.8), extraverted (2.6), playful (2.6), technical (2.2). and nurturing (2.1)."
2. Metric questions that are answered by counting items elicit *ratio* values. You can summarize amounts as a total or an average, such as "The 150 respondents bought 314 models, so the average respondent bought 2.1 models."

2.6 Survey Methods

Most survey researchers prefer telephone interviewing since this data collection method has many strengths and negligible weaknesses. Table 6 compares other methods of data collection to telephone interviewing.

2.7 Sections of a Customer Survey

Researchers have discovered that the most effective customer surveys are organized in this manner:

1. *Introduction.* Usually a survey begins by stating its purpose and sponsor, affirming the value of the respondent's opinions, and promising brevity and confidentiality.
2. *Screener.* The first screening question confirms that the respondent is a customer, while subsequent screening questions make sure the

Table 6. Data-Collection Methods

Methods	Strengths	Weaknesses	Uses
Telephone	Fast Inexpensive Unbiased Nonintrusive Representative	Minimal	Preferred for most uses
Mail	Less expensive No interviewer errors	Slower completion More sampling error More nonresponse error More item nonresponse error	Customer, employee, and membership surveys
On-site meeting	Displays materials Reveals usage behavior Less nonresponse error	More expensive More random sampling error	Low incidence of respondents
Fax	Displays documents	More intrusive More frame error	In conjunction with telephone surveys
Shopper intercept	Displays prototype Tests promotions	More sampling error More interviewer error	Shopping, prototype, and promotional surveys
Kiosk and Internet	Less expensive No interviewer bias	More sampling error More nonresponse error More item nonresponse error	Customer, employee, and membership surveys

respondents fulfill quotas that proportionally represent the important traits of the population of all customers.

3. *Questions about buying behavior.* The first set of survey questions motivates respondents by soliciting suggestions, opinions, and descriptions of their buying behavior.

4. *Psychographic questions.* The next set of questions maintains the respondents' interest in the survey by eliciting self-perceptions.

5. *Demographic questions.* The last set of questions propels respondents to quickly answer the demographic questions and finish the survey.

Eliminate unnecessary questions by only asking decision-oriented questions.

PART II
The 80/20 Rule

CHAPTER 3

The Pareto Distribution

Now that you have reviewed the fundamentals of marketing, you are ready to learn how the 80/20 rule summarizes the Pareto distribution, a universal law that can empower your business. Let us begin by reviewing the life of Pareto and learning about this amazing discovery.

3.1 Discovered by Pareto

Pareto's ancestors were affluent merchants, noblemen, and political agitators from northern Italy. His father was a political exile in France when Vilfredo Frederico Damaso Pareto was born in 1848, the "Year of Revolution." Ten years later his family returned to Italy for his schooling and Pareto graduated in engineering from the Polytechnic Institute of Turin in 1869. His thesis reported on his discovery of an equilibrium theory for solids. Pareto worked many years as a consulting engineer for the government-run railway company, but became an outspoken critic of the Italian government. After inheriting wealth, Pareto quit his position and widely advocated laissez-faire policies such as free trade and open competition. Pareto escaped harassment by government thugs as a political exile in Switzerland and was appointed the professor of political economics at the University of Lausanne in 1892. For decades Pareto wrote seminal treatises on economics, politics, and sociology and influenced European leaders. For example, Benito Mussolini gained political power by espousing Pareto's policies. When Mussolini became a ruthless dictator after World War I, Pareto grew disillusioned by politics and died a broken man in 1923. Afterward, democratic leaders considered Pareto to be Fascist and judged the Pareto distribution to be so unfair that they suppressed knowledge of this universal law.[1]

3.2 Universal and Predictable

Pareto compiled his teaching notes into a book, entitled *Course in Political Economy.*[2] This quantitative book built upon his college thesis by proposing a general equilibrium theory, namely, the distribution of inputs relative to outputs. According to this theory, equilibrium is reached when the top 20% of the inputs generate 80% of the outputs balanced by the bottom 80% of inputs generating 20% of the outputs. The 80/20 rule summarizes the equilibrium point of the Pareto distribution.

3.3 Comparable to a Normal Distribution

Your statistics teacher neglected to teach you about the Pareto distribution (Figure 1), even though it is as valid as the normal "bell-shaped" curve. The distributions are similar since both require a large random sample of numbers, sequence the sample on the *x* axis, and plot amounts on the *y* axis. However, the normal distribution indicates significance, whereas the Pareto distribution predicts outputs.

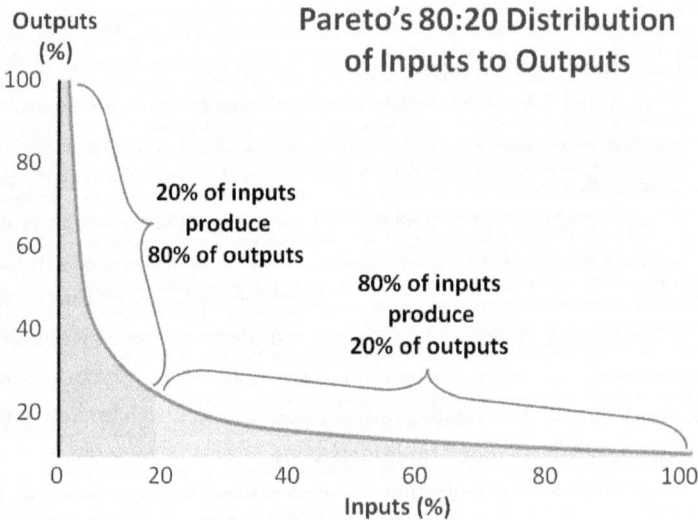

Figure 1. The Pareto distribution.

3.4 Replicated by Research

Pareto's extensive research confirmed that the distribution of inputs to outputs is widely observable, predictable, and logarithmic. More than 50 years after Pareto's discovery, Zipf found that word usage has an 80:20 equilibrium point and called his discovery the *principle of least effort*.[3] In 2006, Newman defined a random sample of numbers as inputs and repeated numbers as outputs and discovered that their relationship replicated the Pareto distribution (Figure 2a) and a log of this distribution approximates a straight line (Figure 2b). Newman noted that this "occurs in an extraordinarily diverse range of phenomena."[4]

3.5 Discussion

Pareto's insights "allow us to forecast unfolding events before they occur."[5] Pareto believed that "if the pie is always going to be sliced unevenly, then the best way to help the poor is by enlarging the pie."[6] The purpose of the book you are reading is to show you how to forecast who will be your most profitable customers, thereby enlarging your pie of profit from customers.

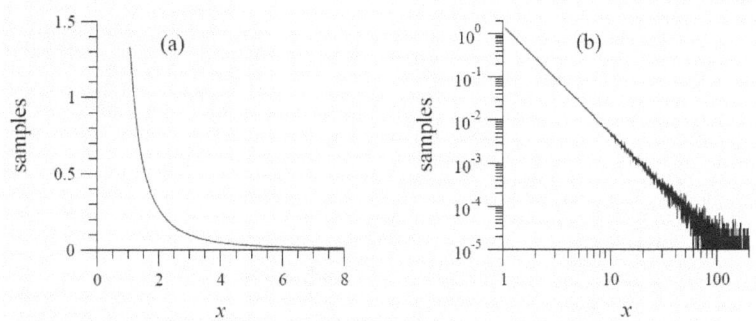

Figure 2. The Pareto distribution (a) and a log of this example (b).

CHAPTER 4

Applications of the 80/20 Rule

4.1 Applications

For over a century, innovative thinkers have used the 80/20 rule to solve practical problems. Table 7 summarizes applications of this universal law to linguistics,[1] quality control,[2] software design,[3] time management,[4] productivity,[5] and human resource management.[6]

4.2 Application to Profit From Customers

A new application of the 80/20 rule increases business profit.

This book explains how you can use the 80/20 rule to increase your profit from customers. You will learn to segment your customers by their profitability and to replace less profitable customers with highly profitable, new customers.

Table 7. Applications of the Pareto Distribution

Years and authors	Affiliations	Applications	Documents and conclusions
1896–97 Vilfredo Pareto	Chair of the Department of Political Economy, Lausanne University	The top 20% of income earners own 80% of the wealth.	*Cours d'Economie Politique* The number of events larger than x is the inverse of x.
1949 George Kingsley Zipf	Professor of Linguistics, Harvard University	The top 20% of effort produces 80% of the results.	*Human Behavior and the Principle of Least Effort* The nth most frequent event occurs $1/n$th as often as the first event.
1951 Joseph Moses Juran	Author with McGraw-Hill	The top 20% of issues cause 80% of the problems.	*Quality Control Handbook* Pareto charts superimpose a cumulative line graph on a declining bar chart.
1964 IBM	Equipment manufacturer (International Business Machines)	The top 20% of software features perform 80% of the operations.	IBM software dominated the industry by creating more efficient software.
1998 Richard Koch	Author with Doubleday	The top 20% of inputs produce 80% of the outputs.	*The 80/20 Principle: The Secret of Achieving More with Less* The 80/20 principle is broadly applicable
2006 Richard Koch	Author with Pritchett	The top 20% of inputs produce 16 times more output than other inputs.	*The Breakthrough Principle of 16×: Real Simple Innovation for 16 Times Better Results* Some inputs are 16 times more effective than others.
2006 Tim Ferriss	Best-selling author with Crown	The bottom 20% of employees cause 80% of the problems.	*The 4-Hour Workweek: Live Anywhere and Join the New Rich* Problems are reduced by eliminating the bottom 20% of employees.
2011 Elizabeth Rush Kruger	Author with Business Expert Press	The top 20% of customers produce 80% of the profit from customers.	*Top Market Strategy: Applying the 80/20 Rule* A top market strategy can quadruple profit from customers.

PART III

Application to Profit from Customers

CHAPTER 5

Segmentation by Profit from Customers

5.1 Overview

Profitability segmentation is the most actionable yet least used type of behavioral segmentation. This approach segments your customers by their profitability and distinguishes your most profitable customers from your least profitable customers.

🔔 **Profitability segmentation can identify the most profitable 20% of your customers and distinguish them from your other customers.**

The results of profitability segmentation show you how to target your most profitable market segment and to position the marketing strategy of your business exclusively for this target market.

🔑 **Your business maximizes its profit from customers by targeting your most profitable customers with marketing strategies.**

5.2 Definition of Profit From Customers

Your heavy users purchase the largest volume of items from your business, but which of your customers generate your highest profit per item? You know from experience that loyal customers are not as price sensitive as disloyal customers. Your loyal customers have *inelastic demand*, so they will continue buying from your business even when your price increases. In contrast, disloyal customers have *elastic demand*, so they tend to buy from your competitors when your price increases. Since your loyal customers can generate a higher potential profit per item than your other customers and your heavy users have the highest *volume of items*, your most profitable customers are your loyal, heavy users.

🔑   **Profit from customers = Profit per item × Volume of items.**

5.3 Current Profitability Segments

If we segment the market of your business by the profitability of its customers, we normally obtain the two market segments shown in Figure 3. The size of each slice indicates the relative size of a market segment, while its color saturation indicates the relative profit from customers in that market segment:

- According to the 80/20 rule, the top 20% of your customers (i.e., your top market segment) generates 80% of your profit from customers. Since your return is four times more than expected (i.e., 80%/20% = 4), we will set the color saturation of this slice at 80% (i.e., 20% × 4 = 80%).

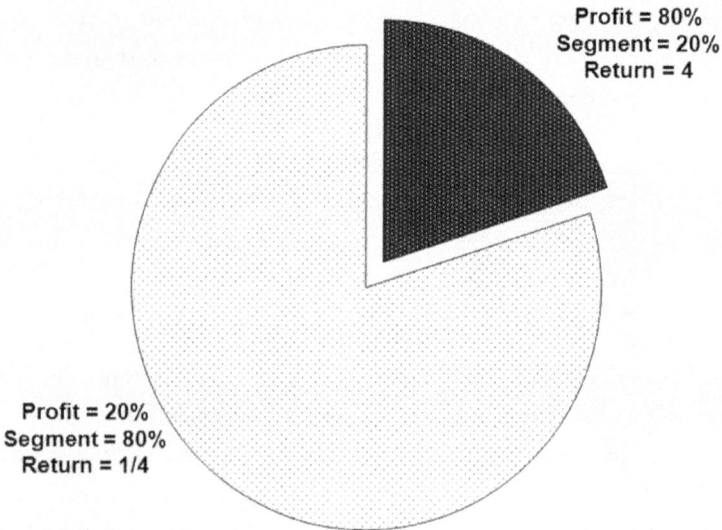

Profit = 80%
Segment = 20%
Return = 4

Profit = 20%
Segment = 80%
Return = 1/4

Figure 3. Current profitability segments.

- The bottom 80% of your customers (i.e., your bottom market segment) generates only 20% of your profit from customers. Since your return is one-fourth (20%/80% = ¼) of your expected profit from customers, we will set its color saturation at 5% (i.e., 20 × 1/4 = 5%).
- Thus your total profit from customers is 80% + 20% = 100%.

The most profitable 20% of your customers are 16 times more profitable than the bottom 80% of your customers (i.e., 4/¼ = 16).

5.4 Profitability With New Customers

Let us see what happens to your profit from customers if you replace customers in your bottom market segment with new customers who are members of your top market segment (Figure 4):

- The top 20% of your customers (your top market segment) would still generate 80% of your prior profit from customers for a fourfold return (i.e., 80%/20% = 4).
- If you replace the bottom 80% of your customers (your bottom market segment) with new customers who are in your top market segment, they would generate 320% of your prior profit from customers (i.e., 4 × 80% = 320%). Thus, your new customers would be 16 times more profitable than the ones they replaced (i.e., 320%/20% = 16).
- Your total profit from customers would now be 80% + 320% = 400%, a fourfold increase (i.e., 400%/100% = 4) over your prior profit from customers.

If your business replaces its less profitable customers with new customers in the top market segment, your profit from customers would quadruple.

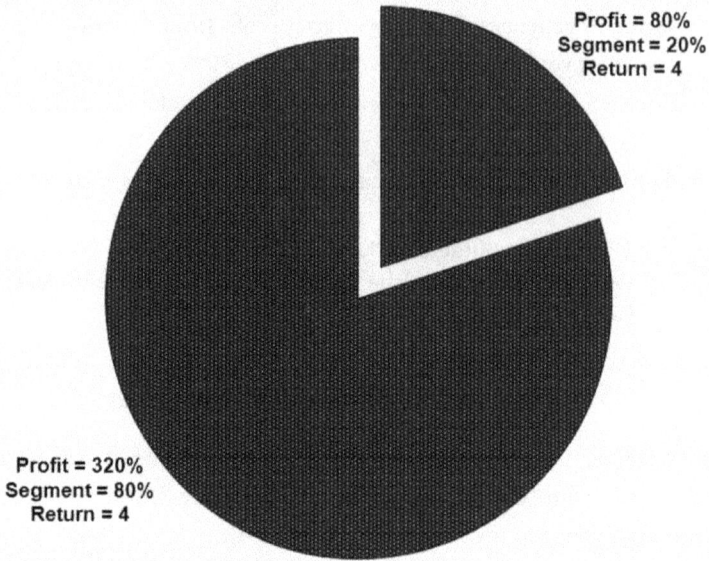

Figure 4. Profitability with new customers.

CHAPTER 6

Steps of Profitability Segmentation

6.1 Conduct Survey Research With Customers

The initial steps of profitability segmentation are similar to survey research with customers. These steps involve interviewing a few diverse customers, creating a customer survey, surveying customers, and analying their overall responses. Part IV and the Appendices demonstrate each step of profitability segmentation with a case example about JetSpray, a fictitious brand of personal watercraft (PWC). For example, the first three chapters in Part IV illustrate the initial steps through fictitious survey research with JetSpray customers. If you are interested in the details, Appendix 1 describes overall JetSpray customers, Appendix 3 specifies the Excel keystrokes that created this report, while Appendix 6 displays the raw data and initial analysis.

6.2 Create Proxy Variables

After the data is collected and summarized, the next step of profitability segmentation is to define proxy variables that represent each customer's volume of items, potential profit per item, and potential profitability. In our fictitious research, the proxy for *volume of items* measures *purchases* while our proxy for *potential profit per item* aggregates loyalty scores into the *loyalty index*. Multiplying *purchases* by the *loyalty index* generates the *profitability index*, our proxy for *potential profit from customers*. For example, Appendix 4 specifies the keystrokes that create these proxy variables with our JetSpray data.

The *profitability index* is *purchases* times the *loyalty index*.

6.3 Segment Your Customers by Their Profitability

Respondents with a certain profitability index score represent all customers in the marketplace with a similar potential for profitability. Chapter 10 explains the essence of profitability segmentation—how to segment JetSpray respondents by their potential profitability, while Appendix 4 specifies the relevant keystrokes.

6.4 Distinguish Your Top Market Segment

We apply the 80/20 rule by defining the *top market segment* as respondents who score in the top 20% on the profitability index.

You can identify new customers just like your highly profitable respondents when you use statistics to profile their distinguishing characteristics. Statistics requires that your sample size be at least 150 respondents so your top market segment will have at least 30 respondents. For your convenience, Chapter 11 explains how to distinguish highly profitable prospects from other prospects, Appendix 2 profiles JetSpray's top market segment, while Appendix 5 specifies the Excel keystrokes used to prepare this report.

The distinguishing characteristics of the top market segment predict which prospects have a high potential for profitability.

6.5 Target Your Top Market Segment
With Your Resources

Target prospects who are similar to respondents in your top market segment.

A successful business evaluates possible market segments and targets segments that fulfill its criteria for a target market. For example, many businesses seek a target market that is identifiable, actionable, underserved, accessible, substantial, growing, and sustainable. Chapter 12 shows how to use distinguishing characteristics to evaluate a top market segment.

According to the 80/20 rule, your business would maximize its profit from customers by focusing resources on serving its top market segment.

6.6 Position Your Business With Marketing Strategies

The distinguishing characteristics of your top market segment suggest effective marketing strategies for serving this target market. Chapter 13 shows how to use this profile to create effective marketing strategies for acquiring highly profitable, new customers. Of course, the profile of JetSpray's top market segment will differ from the profile of your top market segment.

The distinguishing characteristics of your target market suggest effective marketing strategies for attracting highly profitable, new customers to your business.

6.7 Steps to Quadruple Your Profit From Customers

When your business conducts profitability segmentation, specifies research-driven marketing strategies, and fully implements these plans, your business will replace less profitable customers with highly profitable new customers. You can expect that these new customers will be 16 times more profitable than the customers they replace. The next eight chapters illustrate these steps of profitability segmentation (Table 8):

According to the 80/20 rule, targeting new customers like the most profitable 20% of your customers will quadruple your profit from customers.

Table 8. Steps of Profitability Segmentation

1.	Interview 7 to 12 diverse customers in depth.
2.	Create your customer survey based on their responses.
3.	Survey at least 150 proportionally representative customers and analyze their responses.
4.	Segment them by their profitability and define your top market segment as the top 20% of your respondents.

Table 8. Steps of Profitability Segmentation (continued)

5.	Distinguish the characteristics of your top market segment from other market segments.
6.	Evaluate your top market segment and allocate all of your resources to serving this target market.
7.	Create research-driven marketing strategies for acquiring new customers in your top market segment.
8.	Replace the bottom 80% of your customers with these highly profitable, new customers.

How to Increase Profit From Customers

CHAPTER 7

Interview Diverse Customers

Part IV demonstrates the steps of profitability segmentation using a case example about JetSpray, a fictitious brand of personal watercraft. Your first step is conducting in-depth interviews with respondents who represent the diverse demography of your customers. Interview at least seven customers, and continue until their responses become repetitive. Begin your interview

Photo 1. Mrs. Rich Goldman.

by building rapport with the respondent, and continue by asking probing questions to gain insights about the respondent's psychographics and buying behavior. Encourage your respondents to reveal their personality, lifestyle, reputation, values, and media usage, as well as their relationship with your business. Listen intensely as your respondents describe their relationship to your business, such as use, benefits, problems, usage rate, loyalty, shopping priorities, and desires. The following abbreviated example of an in-depth interview (Table 9) demonstrates its spontaneous nature.

Table 9. In-Depth Interview With Mrs. Rich Goldman

Speaker	Transcripts of the in-depth interview
Interviewer	Good morning, Mrs. Goldman. I am delighted to meet you and to talk with you about your JetSpray personal watercraft. You are so gracious to agree to assist us. Your advice will show us how to improve JetSpray. . . . What lovely earrings you are wearing. They're so unique.
Respondent	How kind of you to notice! I inherited these earrings from my great grandmother. She gave land to the city for Goldman Park.
Interviewer	What a generous gift! Does your family enjoy being generous?
Respondent	Oh, yes! We love to host parties at our lake home. We invite members of the country club, the local Rotary Club, our church, the Chamber of Commerce, and other civic groups. They have such a good time at our parties.
Interviewer	What do they like best about your parties?
Respondent	We hire a catering service, but what they most enjoy is riding our JetSprays.
Interviewer	What do you like best about your JetSprays?
Respondent	Our guests can play to their heart's content, and we don't need to worry about their safety.
Interviewer	Tell me more.
Respondent	Our JetSprays have a kill switch, so if they fall off, the JetSpray stops nearby. The craft stays upright so they can easily get back onboard. And then they run the JetSpray up on the beach so others can have a spin. Our JetSprays are the highlight of our parties. All our guests enjoy watching their friends cavort and play around with them.
Interviewer	What makes your guests fall off a JetSpray?

Table 9. In-Depth Interview With Mrs. Rich Goldman (continued)

Speaker	Transcripts of the in-depth interview
Respondent	A passenger falls off when the driver whips the craft around to scare her. The strap across the seat is too tight for a good grip, so she holds onto the driver, but sometimes her grip slips. I wish she could hold on more securely.
Interviewer	Which do you prefer, watching them or riding them?
Respondent	We love to watch our friends ride them, and my husband takes pictures of the riders. We e-mail the photos to them afterwards. They just love the special attention. I've never ridden one myself, but my husband takes care of them before each party. He drives one and pulls the other to the marina to fill up their gas tanks.
Interviewer	Do your children enjoy them?
Respondent	They live so far away that we rarely see our children or grandchildren. Even our grandchildren are adults so they have their own lives.
Interviewer	What else do you enjoy doing?
Respondent	I'm so busy with civic groups and shopping for my home. . . . Did you notice that our lake home appeared in the *Parade of Homes*?
Interviewer	What an honor! Tell me more.
Respondent	The photographer highlighted our JetSprays this year. We've been in the *Parade of Homes* for 9 years. Next year we want to host larger parties, so we need to get a hot dog boat.
Interviewer	Would you like JetSpray to sell hot dog boats?
Respondent	Oh, yes! My husband has looked for one on the Internet, but only resorts and tours can buy them. Besides, we want to buy it from JetSpray since our dealer has given us such great service.
Interviewer	How much do you expect to pay on a hot dog boat?
Respondent	We will spend whatever it takes to have the first hot dog boat on the lake. I'm sure the hot dog boat would make the society page of the newspaper. Everyone would be so jealous of us! That's the best part. . . .
Interviewer	Go on. Our conversation is so fascinating.
Respondent	Oh dear, what have I said? I have nothing more to say. I've already said too much. What I've said is confidential, isn't it?
Interviewer	Of course, your responses will remain confidential. Thanks for helping JetSpray today, Mrs. Goldman! Your insights are so valuable.

CHAPTER 8

Create the Customer Survey

8.1 Summarize Responses

The insights you gain from in-depth interviews will guide you in creating an effective customer survey for your business. Your first step is to summarize and profile the responses from each respondent and then aggregate them in a summary table. For example, Table 10 shows the buyer profile for Mrs. Rich Goldman and Table 11 summarizes the buyer profiles for all 11 in-depth interviewees, starting with her responses. Each duplicated response was used as a response option for a question in Jet-Spray's customer survey (Table 12).

Table 10. Buyer Profile for Mrs. Rich Goldman

Categories	Topics	Characteristics
Buying behaviors	End use	Entertaining guests
	Benefit	Impressing guests
	Usage rate	Two 3-passenger models
	Loyalty	Loyal to manufacturer and dealer
	Shopping priority	Safety features
	Problem	Passengers falling off
	Desire	Hot dog boat
Psychographics	Personality	Extraverted
	Lifestyle	Socializing
	Reputation	Social climber
	Value	Social status
	Media use:	*Parade of Homes*
Demographics	Gender	Female
	Age	60 or older
	Income	Wealthy

Table 11. Summary of JetSpray's In-Depth Interviews (in Three Sections)

ID	Use	Benefit	Seats	Loyalty	Criteria	Problem
1	Guests	Impress	2x3p	1+1+1	Safe	Grip
2	Explore	Share	1x3p	1+0+1	Value	Fall off
3	Guests	Impress	2x3p	1+1+1	Best	Tips
4	Race	Win	1x2p	1+1+0	Fast	Slides
5	Tinker	Learn	2x2p	0+0+0	Price	Stalls
6	Tow	Ski	1x3p	0+0+0	Value	Tips
7	Tinker	Learn	2x2p	0+0+0	Price	Stalls
8	Tow	Ski	1x3p	0+0+0	Value	Tow bar
9	Explore	Share	2x3p	0+1+1	Value	Fall off
10	Guests	Impress	1x3p	1+0+1	Safe	Grip
11	Race	Win	1x2p	0+0+1	Fast	Slides

ID	Desire	Personality	Lifestyle	Attitude	Value
1	Hot Dog	Extravert	Socialite	Snob	Status
2	Cooler	Nurturer	Sharing	View	Nature
3	Larger	Extravert	Sharing	Fun	Status
4	Jump	Competitor	Sports	Win	Skill
5	Storage	Techie	Improve	Make	Ingenuity
6	Larger	Playful	Family	Fun	Freedom
7	Storage	Techie	Improve	Make	Ingenuity
8	Larger	Nurturer	Family	Fun	Freedom
9	Cooler	Playful	Sharing	View	Nature
10	Hot Dog	Extravert	Socialite	Snob	Status
11	Jump	Competitor	Sports	Win	Skill

ID	Media	Sex	Age	Income
1	*Parade of Homes*	Female	60+	Wealthy
2	Waterway chart	Male	50+	Achiever
3	*Parade of Homes*	Male	60+	Wealthy
4	*Extreme Sports*	Male	<30	Struggler
5	*Popular Mechanics*	Male	60+	Striver
6	Situation Comedy	Male	30+	Achiever
7	*Popular Mechanics*	Male	50+	Striver
8	Situation Comedies	Female	<30	Achiever
9	Waterway chart	Female	50+	Wealthy
10	*Parade of Homes*	Female	30+	Wealthy
11	*Extreme Sports*	Male	<30	Striver

Table 12. Response Options for JetSpray's Survey Questions

Topics	Response options
End uses	Compete in races Entertain guests Explore waterways with a passenger Learn to improve engine performance Tow skiers and wakeboarders
Benefits	Feeling free Impressing guests Improving mechanical skills Sharing activities with another Winning races
Types of loyalty	Committed to JetSpray models Committed to a JetSpray dealer Committed to JetSpray equipment
Shopping criteria	Quality Performance Safety Value Price
Problems	Stalling engine Falling off Sliding in sharp turns Tipping with heavy passengers Capsizing
Opportunities	Hot dog boat Garage storage rack Built-in cooler Floating boat jump Larger model for skiing and wakeboarding
Personalities	Competitive Extraverted Nurturing Playful Technical
Activities	Play with my family Compete in extreme sports Improve engine performance Share adventures with another Socialize in groups

Table 12. Response Options for JetSpray's Survey Questions (continued)

Topics	Response options
Reputation	Adventurer Comedian Competitor Self-sufficient person Social climber
Values	Freedom Ingenuity Nature Social status Being the best
Media uses	*Parade of Homes* magazine *Popular Mechanics* magazine Situation comedies on TV Charts of local waterways *Extreme Sports* magazine
Age categories	Under 30 30s 40s 50s 60 or older
Income levels	Struggler Striver Achiever Wealthy
Ownership	Number of models of each size
Gender	Male Female

You are now ready to write a customer survey for your business that is modeled after the survey for JetSpray's customers (Figure 5). Be sure to assign an identification number to each respondent and to terminate unqualified or unneeded respondents.

Respondent ID# _____

Customer Survey   Interviewer ID# _____

Date_____ Time_____

Good morning (afternoon/evening), may I please speak with the woman or man who heads this household?

WHEN THAT PERSON COMES TO THE PHONE, SAY Good morning (afternoon/evening), my name is _____, and I work for JetSpray. We're interested in your opinions of about your **(MODEL)**. JetSpray wants to learn from you how to improve its personal watercraft. This survey is confidential and requires less than 10 minutes of your time.

IF REFUSAL, SAY Would another time be better for you? **SET TIME** _____

Screener

S-1 Do you currently own personal watercraft by JetSpray?

( ) 1. Yes **CONTINUE TO S-2.**

( ) 2. No **THANK AND TERMINATE.**

S-2 How many *two*-passenger models by JetSpray have you ever purchased new?

( )   **RECORD NUMBER.**

THANK AND TERMINATE IF QUOTA IS FULL.

S-3 How many *three*-passenger models by JetSpray have you ever purchased new?

( )   **RECORD NUMBER.**

THANK AND TERMINATE IF QUOTA IS FULL.

THANK AND TERMINATE IF NO MODELS WERE PURCHASED.

S-4 Do you live in a county with a coastline?

( ) 1. Yes, I live near an ocean.

THANK AND TERMINATE IF QUOTA IS FULL.

( ) 2. No, I live inland.

THANK AND TERMINATE IF QUOTA IS FULL.

Figure 5. Survey of JetSpray's customers.

Survey

1. Which problems do you have with your JetSpray? **CHECK ALL THAT APPLY.**
    ( ) 1. Stalling engine
    ( ) 2. Falling off
    ( ) 3. Sliding in sharp turns
    ( ) 4. Tipping with heavy passengers
    ( ) 5. Capsizing

2. What improvements do you want JetSpray to make? **CHECK ALL THAT APPLY.**
    ( ) 1. Hot dog boat
    ( ) 2. Garage storage rack
    ( ) 3. Built-in cooler
    ( ) 4. Floating boat jump
    ( ) 5. Larger model for skiing and wake boarding

3. Are you a loyal customer? Are you committed to . . . **CHECK ALL THAT APPLY.**
    ( ) 1. JetSpray models
    ( ) 2. A JetSpray dealer
    ( ) 3. JetSpray equipment

   I'm going to describe ways that you may relate to your JetSpray. Please indicate how strongly you agree or disagree with each statement using this rating scale: 1 is *strongly disagree*, 2 is *disagree*, 3 is *neutral*, 4 is *agree*, and 5 is *strongly agree*.
   REPEAT THE RATING SCALE AS NEEDED.

4. I use my JetSpray to . . .
    ( ) 1 2 3 4 5   Compete in races
    ( ) 1 2 3 4 5   Entertain guests
    ( ) 1 2 3 4 5   Explore waterways with a passenger
    ( ) 1 2 3 4 5   Learn to improve engine performance
    ( ) 1 2 3 4 5   Tow skiers and wake boarders

Figure 5. Survey of JetSpray's customers (continued).

5. I benefit from my JetSpray by . . .

(   ) 1 2 3 4 5   Feeling free

(   ) 1 2 3 4 5   Impressing guests

(   ) 1 2 3 4 5   Improving mechanical skills

(   ) 1 2 3 4 5   Sharing adventures

(   ) 1 2 3 4 5   Winning races

6. When I bought a personal watercraft, I shopped for the best . . .

(   ) 1 2 3 4 5   Quality

(   ) 1 2 3 4 5   Performance

(   ) 1 2 3 4 5   Safety features

(   ) 1 2 3 4 5   Value

(   ) 1 2 3 4 5   Price

7. How well does each statement describe you? My personality is . . .

(   ) 1 2 3 4 5   Competitive

(   ) 1 2 3 4 5   Extraverted

(   ) 1 2 3 4 5   Nurturing

(   ) 1 2 3 4 5   Playful

(   ) 1 2 3 4 5   Technical

8. I love to . . .

(   ) 1 2 3 4 5   Play with my family

(   ) 1 2 3 4 5   Compete in extreme sports

(   ) 1 2 3 4 5   Improve engines

(   ) 1 2 3 4 5   Share activities with another

(   ) 1 2 3 4 5   Socialize in groups

9. People who know me say I am a(n) . . .

(   ) 1 2 3 4 5   Adventurer

(   ) 1 2 3 4 5   Comedian

(   ) 1 2 3 4 5   Competitor

(   ) 1 2 3 4 5   Self-sufficient person

(   ) 1 2 3 4 5   Social climber

Figure 5. Survey of JetSpray's customers (continued).

10. I certainly value . . .

( ) 1 2 3 4 5   Freedom

( ) 1 2 3 4 5   Ingenuity

( ) 1 2 3 4 5   Nature

( ) 1 2 3 4 5   Social status

( ) 1 2 3 4 5   Being the best

11. I truly enjoy . . .

( ) 1 2 3 4 5   *Parade of Homes* magazine

( ) 1 2 3 4 5   *Popular Mechanics* magazine

( ) 1 2 3 4 5   Situation comedies on TV

( ) 1 2 3 4 5   Waterway charts

( ) 1 2 3 4 5   *Extreme Sports* magazine

12. What is your age level?

( ) 1. Under 30

( ) 2. 30s

( ) 3. 40s

( ) 4. 50s

( ) 5. 60 or older

13. Let's skip the income question. Would you describe yourself as a . . . ?

( ) 1. Struggler

( ) 2. Striver

( ) 3. Achiever

( ) 4. Wealthy person

14. RECORD GENDER

( ) 1. Male

( ) 2. Female

Thank you for completing this survey.

Figure 5. Survey of JetSpray's customers (continued).

CHAPTER 9

Survey Customers and Analyze Responses

9.1 Quota Sampling

We selected quota sampling to ensure that our sample proportionally represented the population of JetSpray customers on the two most important characteristics, model size and location. JetSpray's sales records indicated that the owners bought the two model sizes equally, so half of the respondents must own a two-passenger model and the other half must own a three-passenger model. Those who own both sizes can fulfill either model-size quota. JetSpray's sales records indicated that 60% of the respondents live inland while 40% live in a county bordered by a coastline. Table 13 breaks down our sample of 150 respondents into quotas for the four subgroups, namely, coastal owners of three-passenger models, coastal owners of two-passenger models, inland owners of three-passenger models, and inland owners of two-passenger models. These quotas must match the actual percentage of the population in each subgroup.

Table 13. Quotas for JetSpray's Respondents

| Model size | Location | | | | Total | |
| | Coastal | | Inland | | | |
	%	#	%	#	%	#
Three-passengers	20	30	30	45	50	75
Two-passengers	20	30	30	45	50	75
Total	**40**	**60**	**60**	**90**	**100**	**150**

9.2 Analysis of Customer Responses

Appendix 1 describes overall JetSpray customers, Appendix 2 specifies the Excel keystrokes used to prepare this report, while Appendix 6 shows the data and initial analysis in an Excel worksheet. The report on overall JetSpray customers was prepared by following these steps:

1. Code and enter the responses of each respondent.
2. Count the responses to each survey item, and aggregate their purchases.
3. Confirm the fulfillment of the quotas.
4. Calculate percentages for nonmetric items.
5. Calculate averages for metric items.
6. Compile these percentages and averages into tables for the report.
7. Pivot the tables into bar charts.
8. Outline your report, state each survey question, and insert the bar charts.
9. Summarize the results in descending order, and insert these results after the relevant questions.

CHAPTER 10

Define the Profitability Segments

Appendix 2 compares highly profitable customers with other customers in the report on JetSpray's top market segment, while Appendix 6 shows how to append proxy variables to the data in an Excel worksheet. Appendix 4 specifies the keystrokes for defining the profitability segments with the following steps:

1. Define *purchases* as the proxy for *volume of items*, and calculate each respondent's purchases.
2. Define the *loyalty index* as the proxy for *potential profit per item*, and determine each respondent's score on the loyalty index.
3. Define the *profitability index* as the proxy for *potential profit from customers*, and multiply purchases by the loyalty index to determine each respondent's score on the profitability index.
4. Sort respondents in descending order by their profitability index scores, as shown in Figure 6.
5. Define the *top market segment* as the 20% of respondents with the highest profitability index scores, and set the breakpoints for the profitability segments (Table 14).
6. Chart the profitability segments (Figure 7).
7. Create a pie chart of the profitability segments (Figure 8).

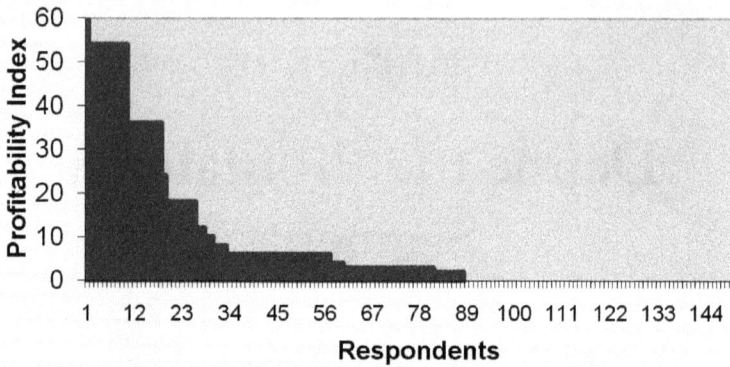

Figure 6. Profitability of JetSpray's respondents.

Table 14. Breakpoints for JetSpray's Market Segments

Profitability index scores	Number of respondents	Cumulative percentages	Profitability segments
0	62	41	Bottom market segment
2	7	46	Middle market segment
3	21	60	
4	3	62	
6	24	78	
8	3	80	
9	0	80	
10	2	81	Top market segment
12	2	83	
18	7	87	
24	1	88	
36	8	93	
54	9	99	
60	1	100	

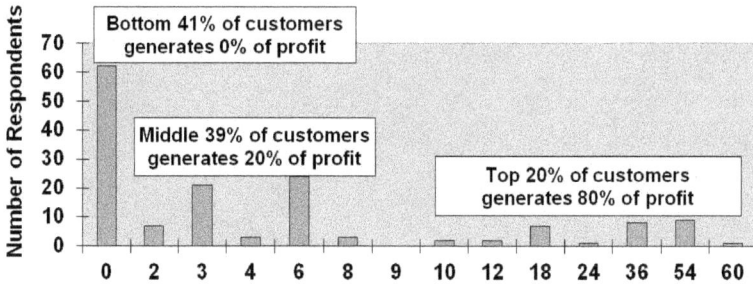

Figure 7. Profitability index scores for JetSpray's market segments.

CHAPTER 11

Distinguish the Top Market Segment

Appendix 2 profiles customers with high potential profitability in the report on JetSpray's top market segment, while Appendix 5 specifies the keystrokes used to distinguish customers in the top market segment from other customers. Appendix 6 shows how to statistically compare these two groups in a Microsoft Excel worksheet using these steps:

1. Calculate the percentage of responses for each nonmetric item with both groups: the top market segment and other customers.
2. Compare these percentages to test whether they are significantly different for the two groups.
3. Calculate the average response for each metric item with both groups.
4. Compare these averages to test whether they are significantly different for the two groups.
5. Compile these percentages and averages into tables for the report.
6. Pivot the tables into bar charts.
7. Outline your report, state each survey question, and insert the bar charts.
8. Summarize the results in descending order, mark significant differences between the groups, and insert these results after relevant questions.
9. Compile the significant distinctions as a buyer's profile for the Jet-Spray's top market segment (Table 15).

Table 15. Buyer Profile for JetSpray's Top Market Segment

Categories	Topics	Profile of JetSpray customers in the top market segment
Buying behavior	End use	Entertaining guests
	Benefit	Impressing guests
	Usage rate	Two 3-passenger models
	Loyalty	JetSpray models, a dealer, and equipment
	Shopping criteria	Safety features and quality
	Problem	Tipping and falling off
	Desire	Built-in cooler and hot dog boat
Psychographics	Personality	Extraverted
	Lifestyle	Socialize in groups
	Reputation	Social climber
	Value	Social status
	Media	*Parade of Homes* and comedies on TV
Demographics	Location	Inland
	Gender	Female
	Age	50s
	Income	Wealthy

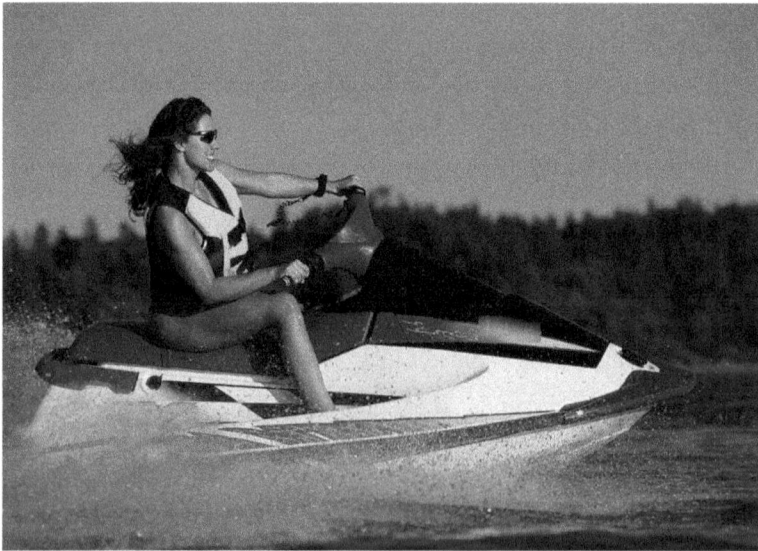

Photo 2. Side view of a JetSpray.

CHAPTER 12

Evaluate and Target the Top Market Segment

12.1 Evaluate JetSpray's Top Market Segment

Most businesses seek a target market that is identifiable, actionable, underserved, accessible, substantial, growing, and sustainable. Table 16 evaluates the top market segment relative to these seven criteria. The evaluation comprises statistically significant characteristics that distinguish customers in the top market segment from other customers. Based upon this evaluation, we conclude that JetSpray's top market segment fulfills each of the seven criteria and thereby qualifies as JetSpray's target market.

Table 16. Evaluation of JetSpray's Top Market Segment

Criteria	Evaluation of the top market segment
Identifiable	Members of the top market segment are identified as wealthy, extraverted, female, social climbers in their 50s who live inland; socialize in groups; and value social status.
Actionable	These customers seek distinctive marketing strategies since they use JetSprays to entertain and impress guests; shop for safety features and quality; worry about their guests tipping and falling off; and desire a built-in cooler and a hot dog boat.
Underserved	We assume they are underserved since competitors probably target typical customers. In contrast with the top market segment, other customers are self-sufficient, striving, and youthful males who share activities; enjoy competitions; value freedom; and worry about a stalling engine.
Accessible	Members of the top market strategy can be accessed through the *Parade of Homes,* situation comedies on TV, and direct marketing campaigns.
Substantial	According to the 80/20 rule, we expect customers in the top market segment to return 16 times more profit than other customers.

Table 16. Evaluation of JetSpray's Top Market Segment (continued)

Criteria	Evaluation of the top market segment
Growing	We assume this market is growing since baby boomers are reaching their 50s and females are buying more recreational vehicles.
Sustainable	Based upon the above analysis, we assume this criterion will also be fulfilled.

12.2 Target Your Top Market Segment

When your business focuses its time, money, and marketing strategies on targeting its top market segment, it will attract more of these highly profitable customers (Table 17). However, your business will suffer an opportunity cost unless it switches its resources away from serving other market segments.

> An *opportunity cost* is the amount of profit that could have been earned by using resources more effectively.

Table 17. Resource Allocation to Profitability Segments

Profitability segment	Score on the Profitability Index	Decision logic
Bottom market segment	Low score	These customers tend to be opportunists who will switch brands for a better price. Avoid using price-cutting tactics such as rebates, coupons, or special offers, since these sales promotions cost money, cut the profit per item, and lower customer perceptions of your brand's value.
Middle market segment	Moderate score	Serving this market segment dilutes your profit and bogs down your resources. Your business will encounter an opportunity cost unless it focuses all resources on serving the top market segment.
Top market segment	Top 20% of scores	These loyal customers tolerate high prices, so your business can earn a high profit per item. In addition, they are heavy users of your business. According to the 80/20 rule, members of the top market segment produce 80% of your profit and return 16 times more profit than your other customers.

🔔 Avoid the bottom market segment since these customers are much less profitable than customers in your top market segment.

🔔 Ignore the middle market segment so you do not dilute your focus from serving your top market segment.

🔔 Target your top market segment with your resources so your business will maximize its profit from customers.

CHAPTER 13

Create Research-Driven Marketing Strategies

13.1 JetSpray's Marketing Strategies

The results of profitability segmentation provide valuable insights about the distinguishing characteristics of JetSpray's top market segment. These insights guided the author in creating marketing strategies to attract highly profitable new customers (Table 18). However, your results from the profitability segmentation of your business will guide you to create entirely different marketing strategies.

Table 18. Marketing Strategies for JetSpray's Target Market Segment

Marketing tools	Marketing elements	Marketing strategies
Design the product for status.	Brand name	Build a reputation for status.
	Style	Create an elitist look.
	Features	Improve grip and stability; build in a cooler
	Quality	Warranty the safety of JetSprays.
	Labeling	Provide a customized nameplate.
	New product	Offer a hot dog boat for several riders.
Price for high profit per item.	Retail price	Set the highest retail price.
	Free services	Provide free training and insurance.
	Lease	Make it deductible as a business expense.
	Bundling	Price JetSprays in pairs.
	Trade-ins	Pay generously for trading in old models.
Sell in multiples.	Orders	Offer custom colors and designs.
	Referrals	Obtain referrals upon delivery.
	Bonus	Pay a bonus for multiple and repeat purchases.

Table 18. Marketing Strategies for JetSpray's Target Market Segment (continued)

Marketing tools	Marketing elements	Marketing strategies
Promote to the target market.	Motivation	Appeal to the desire for social status
	Ad heading	"Impress your guests with JetSprays."
	Ad graphic	Show a hostess waving at JetSpray riders.
	Media for ad	*Parade of Homes* and society page of local newspapers.
	Publicity	Write articles on hosting a JetSpray party.
	Internet	Release funny videos about JetSpray riders.
	Contact list	Target wealthy, middle-aged people who live on a lake.
	Publicity	Sponsor high-status society events.

CHAPTER 14

Quadruple Profit From Customers

14.1 JetSpray's Current Profit From Customers

Figure 8 shows JetSpray's *initial* profitability segments. Evidently, customers in JetSpray's top market segment generate about eight times more profit than those in its middle market segment, and infinitely more than customers in its bottom market segment:

- Customers in the top market segment *(i.e., the top 20%) generate four times* the expected profit.
- Customers in the middle market segment (i.e. the middle 39%) generate about one-half of the expected profit.
- Customers in the bottom market segment (i.e., the bottom 41%) generate no profit.

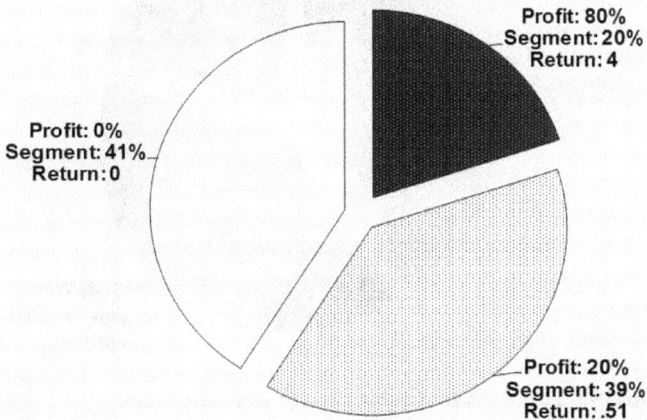

Figure 8. Current profitability of JetSpray's market segments.

14.2 JetSpray's Profitability With New Customers

Figure 9 shows JetSpray's profitability segments after conducting profitability segmentation and fully implementing marketing strategies that
focus on the top market segment. You can clearly see why your profit
from customers will quadruple when your business replaces its less profitable customers with highly profitable, new customers.

- Customers in top market (i.e., the top 20%) still quadruple the
  expected profit (i.e., 20% × 4 = 80% of the previous total profit
  from customers).

- New customers in the top market segment now replace the 80% of
  the customers in the lower market segments, so they quadruple the
  expected profit (i.e., 80% × 4 = 320% of the previous total profit
  from customers).

- As a result, JetSpray's *total profit* will quadruple (i.e., 80% + 320% =
  400% of the previous total profit from customers).

🔔 The profit from customers will quadruple by replacing less
profitable customers with highly profitable, new customers.

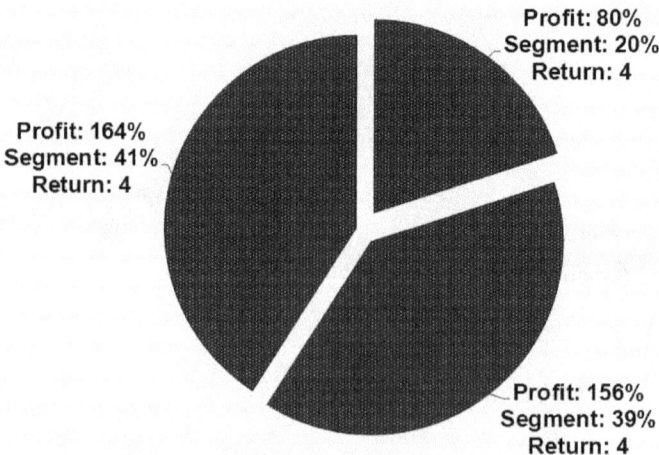

Profit: 80%
Segment: 20%
Return: 4

Profit: 164%
Segment: 41%
Return: 4

Profit: 156%
Segment: 39%
Return: 4

Figure 9. JetSpray's profitability with new customers.

Appendixes

Photo 3.   Front view of a JetSpray.

APPENDIX 1

Report on Overall JetSpray Customers

Methodology

JetSpray conducted 11 in-depth interviews with demographically diverse customers to identify responses options for a customer survey. Then JetSpray administered the customer survey to 150 proportionally representative customers by telephone. This report uses percentages or averages to summarize their overall responses to each survey question and lists these results in sequential order.

A1.1 Demographics (Items S-4 and 12–14)

Quotas. Quotas required that 60% of the respondents live inland, whereas 40% live in a county with a coastline. Half of the respondents owned a two-passenger model, but 57% of the respondents owned a three-passenger model since 7% owned both model sizes.

Gender and Age. Overall, about two-thirds (65%) of JetSpray owners are male. Their age levels are bimodal with 28% under 30, 10% in their 30s, 17% in their 40s, and almost half (45%) at least 50 years old (Chart 1).

Income Level. Many JetSpray owners (62%) consider themselves a struggler or striver, but only 38% consider themselves an achiever or wealthy person (Chart 2).

1: Age Distribution

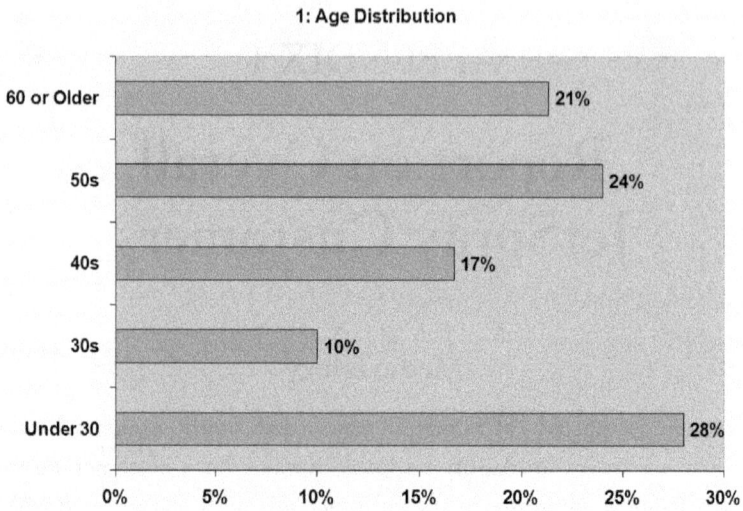

Chart 1. *Age distribution.*

2: Income Level

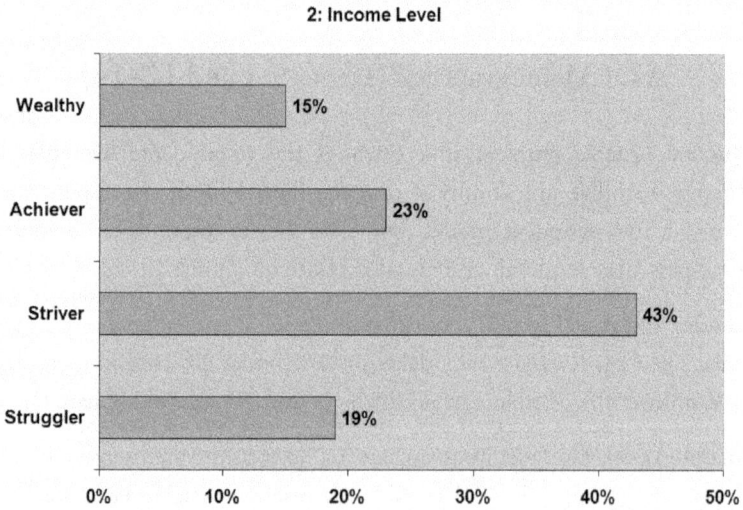

Chart 2. *Income level.*

A1.2 Psychographics (Items 7–11)

The respondents rated their level of agreement with the following descriptive statements on a 5-point Likert rating scale. The report lists in descending order their average rating for each statement.

Personality. *My personality is . . . competitive, extraverted, playful, technical, or nurturing* (Chart 3).

Activity Loved. *I love to . . . share activities, socialize in groups, play with my family, compete in extreme sports, or improve engines* (Chart 4).

Reputation. *People who know me say I am a . . . self-sufficient person, competitor, adventurer, social climber, or comedian* (Chart 5).

Value. *I certainly value . . . freedom, being the best, ingenuity, nature, or social status* (Chart 6).

Media Enjoyed. *I truly enjoy . . . situation comedies on TV,* Popular Mechanics *magazine,* Extreme Sports *magazine, charts of local waterways, or* Parade of Homes *magazine* (Chart 7).

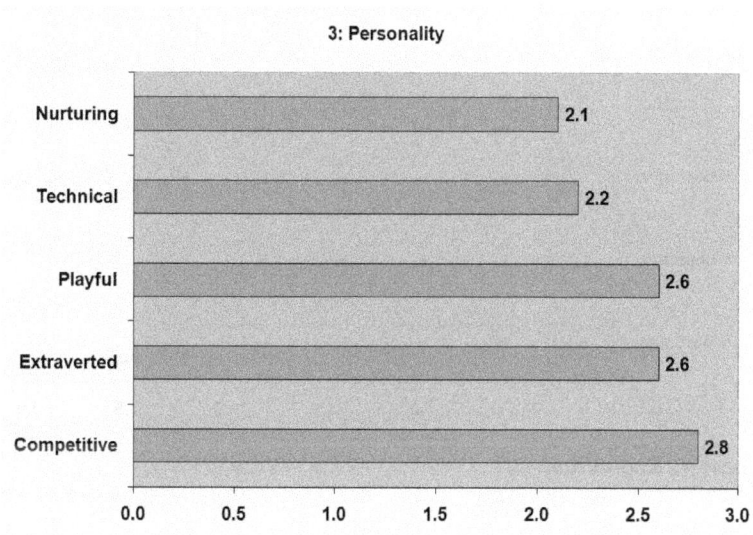

3: Personality

Personality	Rating
Nurturing	2.1
Technical	2.2
Playful	2.6
Extraverted	2.6
Competitive	2.8

Chart 3. Personality.

4: Activity Loved

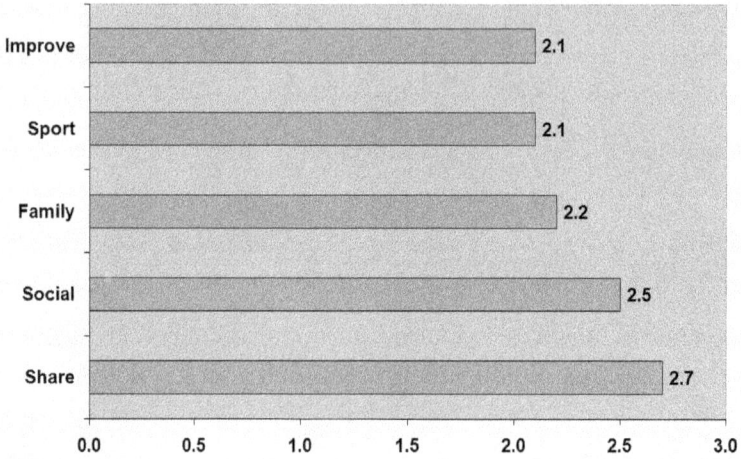

Chart 4. Activity loved.

5: Reputation

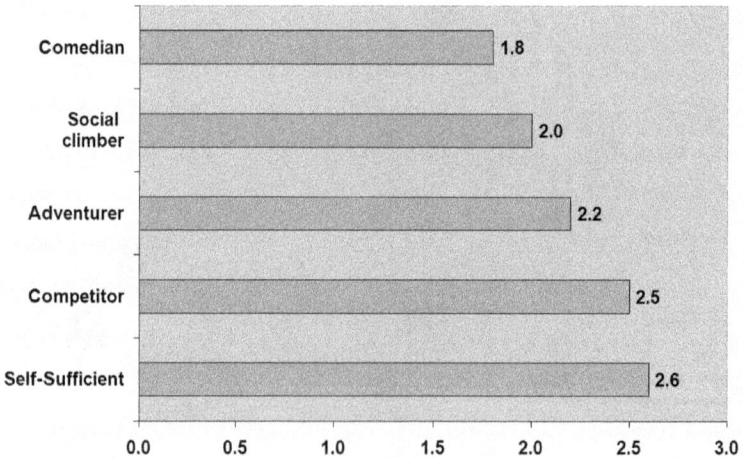

Chart 5. Reputation.

6: Values

Value	Score
Status	2.3
Nature	2.4
Ingenuity	2.5
Best	2.8
Freedom	2.8

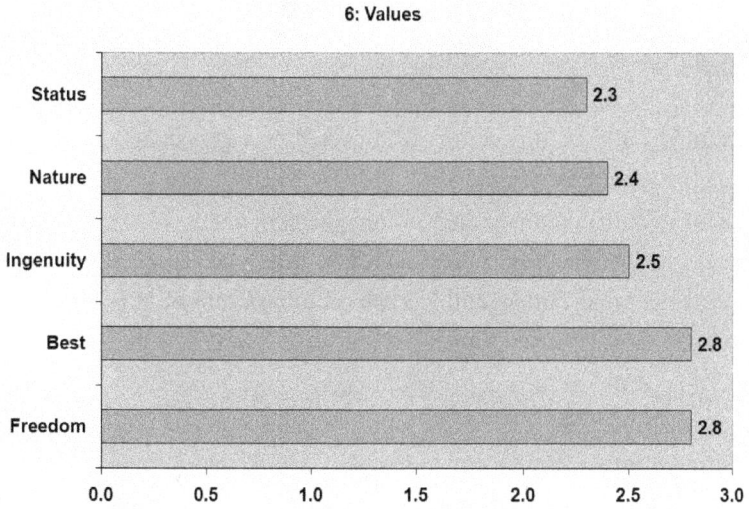

Chart 6. Values.

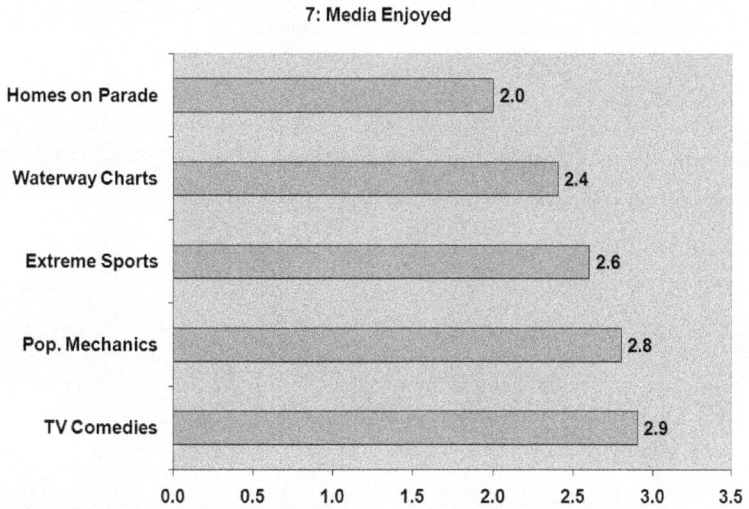

7: Media Enjoyed

Media	Score
Homes on Parade	2.0
Waterway Charts	2.4
Extreme Sports	2.6
Pop. Mechanics	2.8
TV Comedies	2.9

Chart 7. Media enjoyed.

A1.3 Buying Behavior (Items S-2, S-3, and 1–6)

Purchases. The 150 respondents bought 314 JetSprays over their life-time, so the average JetSpray owner bought 2.1 models. Of these, 143 (46%) are two-passenger models, and 171 (54%) are three-passenger models. Overall, 18% bought one small (i.e., two-passenger) model, 31% bought two small models, and 5% bought more than two small models. In addition, 26% bought one large (i.e., three-passenger) model, 11% bought two large models, and 9% bought more than two large models or a combination of model sizes.

Problems. *Which problems do you have with your JetSpray . . . stalling engine, tipping with heavy passengers, falling off, sliding in sharp turns, or capsizing* (Chart 8)?

Desires. *What improvements do you want JetSpray to make . . . built-in cooler, garage storage rack, larger model for skiing and wake boarding, float-ing boat jump, or hot dog boat* (Chart 9)?

Loyalty. *Are you a loyal customer? I am committed to JetSpray . . . models* (41%), *a dealer* (28%), *or equipment* (19%). Overall, 59% reported at least one type of loyalty to JetSpray (Chart 10).

Criteria. *When I bought a personal watercraft, I shopped for the best . . . performance, safety features, price, value, or quality* (Chart 11).

Usage. *I use my JetSpray to . . . entertain guests, explore waterways, com-pete in races, improve engine performance, or tow skiers and wake boarders* (Chart 12).

Benefits. *I benefit from my JetSpray by . . . feeling free, sharing adventures, improving mechanical skills, impressing guests, or winning races* (Chart 13).

8: Problems

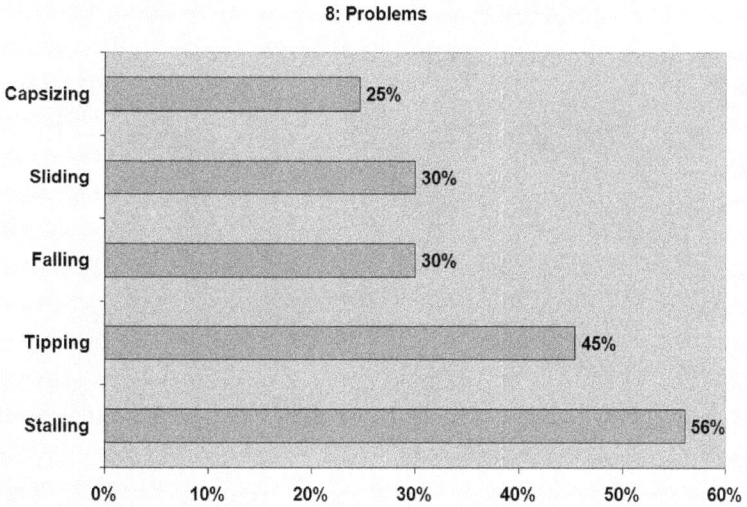

Chart 8. Problems.

9: Desires

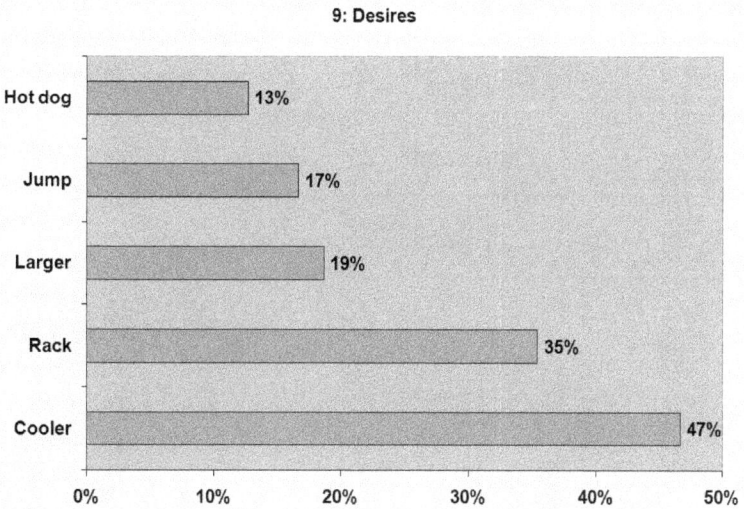

Chart 9. Desires.

10: Loyalty

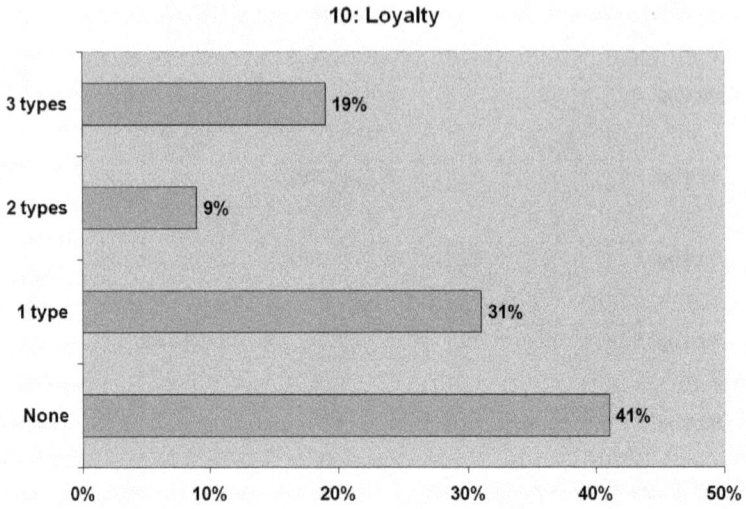

Chart 10. *Loyalty.*

11: Criteria

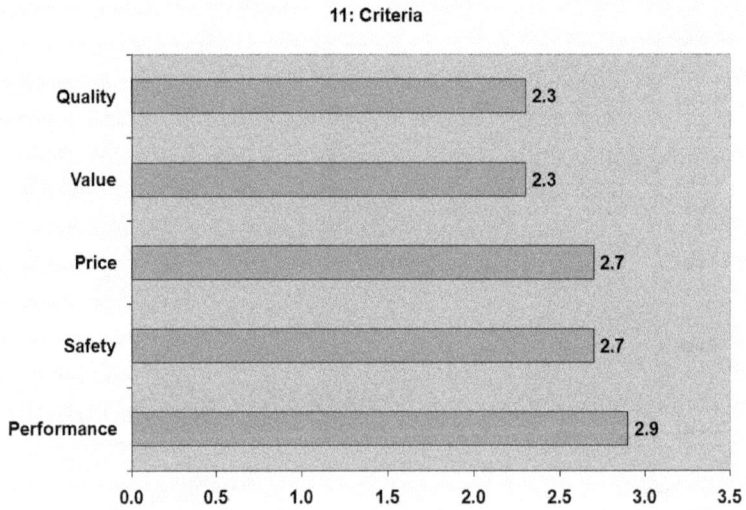

Chart 11. *Criteria.*

12: Usage

Category	Value
Tow	2.2
Learn	2.3
Compete	2.3
Explore	2.4
Entertain	2.5

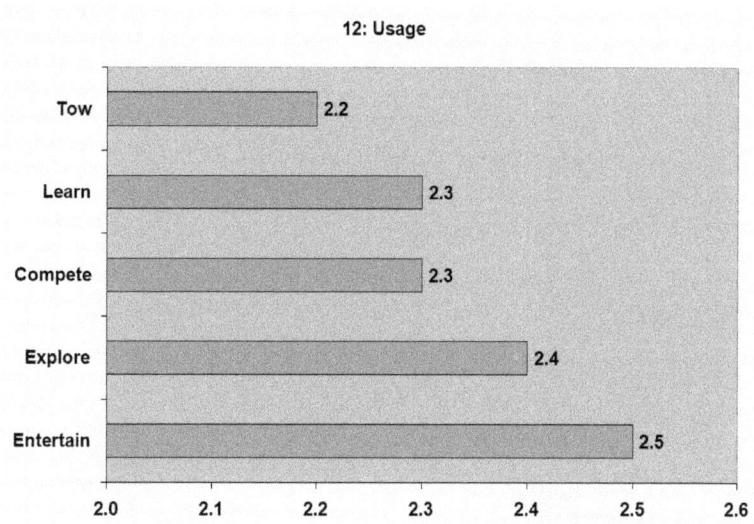

Chart 12. Usage.

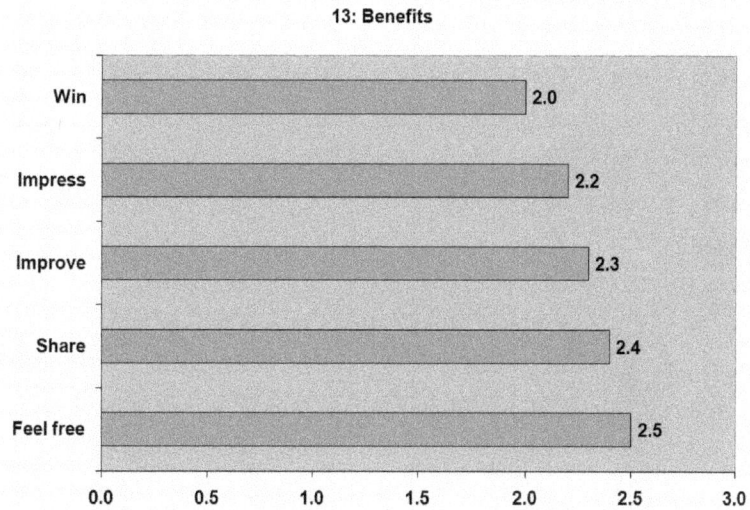

13: Benefits

Category	Value
Win	2.0
Impress	2.2
Improve	2.3
Share	2.4
Feel free	2.5

Chart 13. Benefits.

APPENDIX 2

Report on JetSpray's Top Market Segment

Methodology

JetSpray defined a proxy for potential profit from customers, sorted the respondents by this measure, and grouped the most profitable 20% of the respondents into the top market segment. Percentages and averages summarize the responses of customers in the top market segment (i.e., target market) and other customers. This report identifies statistically significant differences between these two groups and lists the results in sequential order from the perspective of the top market segment.

A2.1 Demographics (Items S-4, 12–14)

Quotas. Compared to other customers, significantly more in the target market live inland (87% versus 53%) and have purchased three-passenger models (65% versus 52%).

Gender and Age. The target market has significantly more females (70% versus 27%), more in their 50s (53% versus 17%), and fewer under 30 years of age (10% versus 33%) than other market segments (Chart 14).

Income. In contrast to others customers, significantly more of the target market consider themselves a wealthy person (53% versus 6%), and fewer consider themselves a striver (3% versus 53%) (Chart 15).

14: Target Market's Age

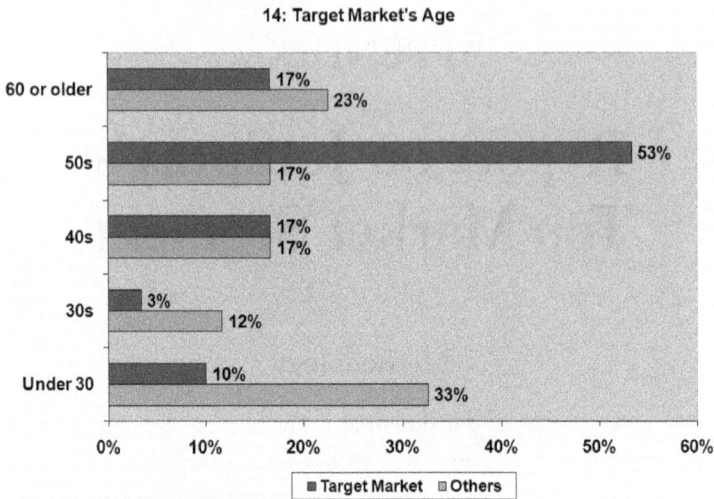

Chart 14. *Target market's age.*

15: Target Market's Income

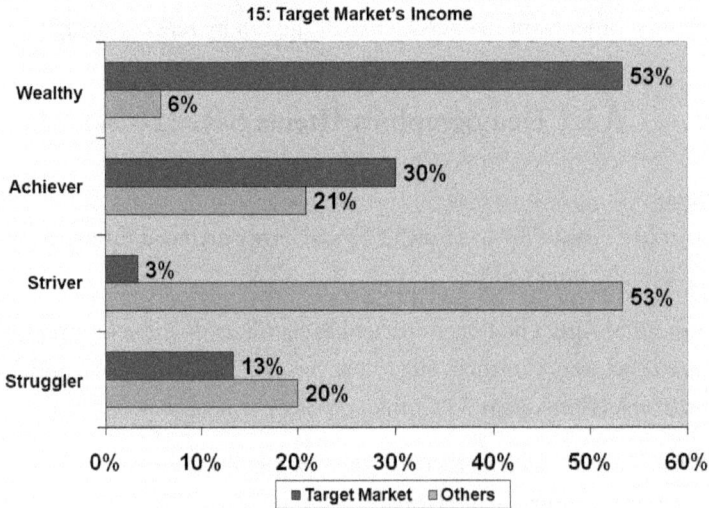

Chart 15. *Target market's income.*

A2.2 Psychographics (Items 7–11)

The respondents in the target market and other respondents rated their agreement with the following descriptive statements on a 5-point Likert rating scale. For each item, we compared the average rating of the two groups using the *t*-test of the difference between group means. An asterisk (*) indicates a statistically significant difference between these two groups.

Personality. *My personality is . . . extraverted,* rather than competitive,* playful,* nurturing, or technical* (Chart 16).

Activities. *I love to . . . socialize in groups* and share activities, rather than play with my family, improve engines,* or compete in extreme sports* (Chart 17).

Reputation. *People who know me say I am a . . . social climber,* rather than a competitor, self-sufficient person,* adventurer,* or comedian* (Chart 18).

Value. *I certainly value . . . social status,* rather than being the best,* nature, freedom,* or ingenuity* (Chart 19).

Media. *I truly enjoy . . .* Parade of Homes *magazine* and situation comedies on TV,* rather than charts of local waterways,* Extreme Sports *magazine,* or* Popular Mechanics* *magazine* (Chart 20).

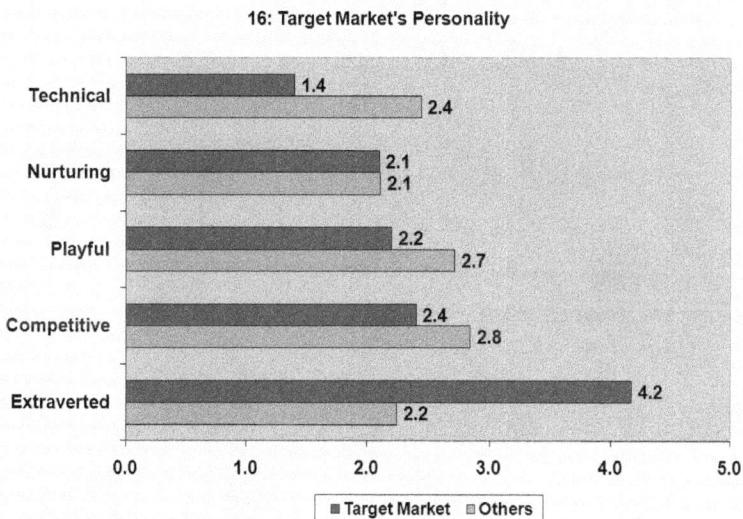

Chart 16. Target market's personality.

17: Target Market's Activities

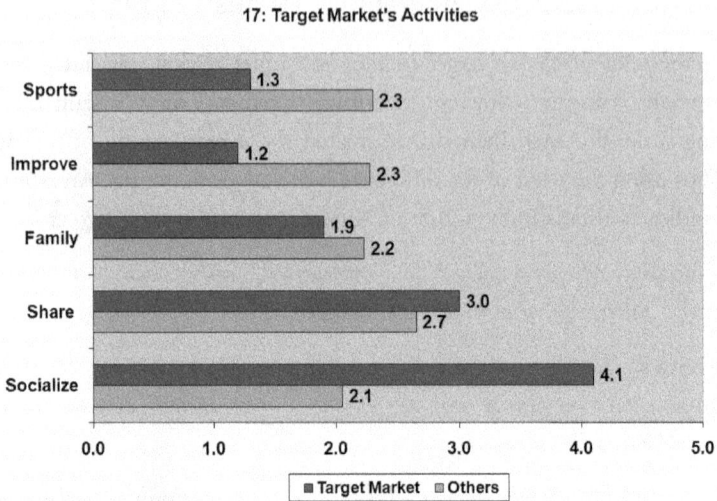

Chart 17. *Target market's activities.*

18: Target Market's Reputation

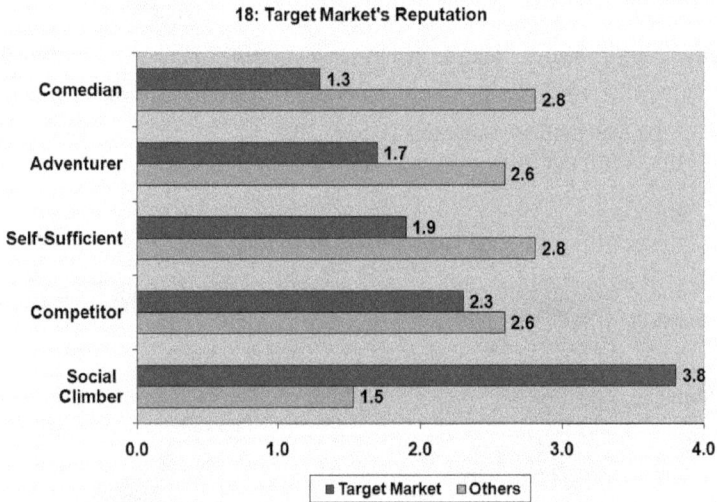

Chart 18. *Target market's reputation.*

19: Target Market's Values

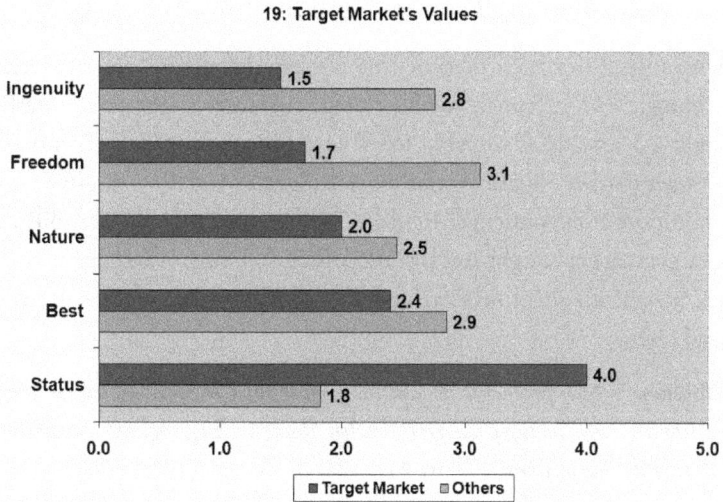

Chart 19. *Target market's values*.

20: Target Market's Media

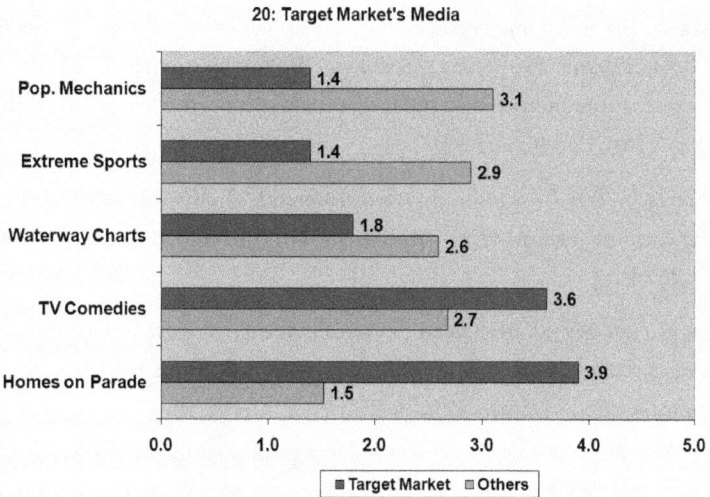

Chart 20. *Target market's media*.

A2.3 Buying Behavior (Items S-2, S-3, 1–6)

Ownership. Over their lifetime, the 30 respondents in the target market bought 134 JetSprays, so the average customer in the target market bought 4.5 models. Compared to other customers, significantly more in the target market bought two or more JetSprays (100% versus 46%) and two or more three-passenger models (70% versus 16%). In fact, 30% of the target market bought six large models, 27% bought two large models, 20% bought six small models, and 23% bought other combinations of model sizes.

Problems. *Which problems do you have with your JetSpray . . . falling off* and tipping with heavy passengers, rather than stalling engine,* capsizing,* or sliding in sharp turns** (Chart 21)?

Desires. *What improvements do you want JetSpray to make . . . a built-in cooler and hot dog boat,* rather than a garage storage rack,* floating boat jump,* or larger model for skiing and wake boarding** (Chart 22)?

Loyalty. *Are you a loyal customer? I am committed to JetSpray . . . models** (100%), *a dealer** (93%), *or equipment** (93%). Compared to others, significantly more members of the target market reported loyalty to all three (93% versus 1%) (Chart 23).

Criteria. *When I bought a personal watercraft, I shopped for the best . . . safety features* and quality,* rather than for performance,* value,* or price** (Chart 24).

Usage. *I use my JetSpray to . . . entertain guests,* not tow skiers and wake boarders, explore waterways with a passenger,* compete in races,* or learn to enhance motor performance** (Chart 25).

Benefits. *I benefit from my JetSpray by . . . impressing guests,* rather than by sharing adventures,* feeling free,* winning races,* or improving mechanical skills** (Chart 26).

21: Target Market's Problems

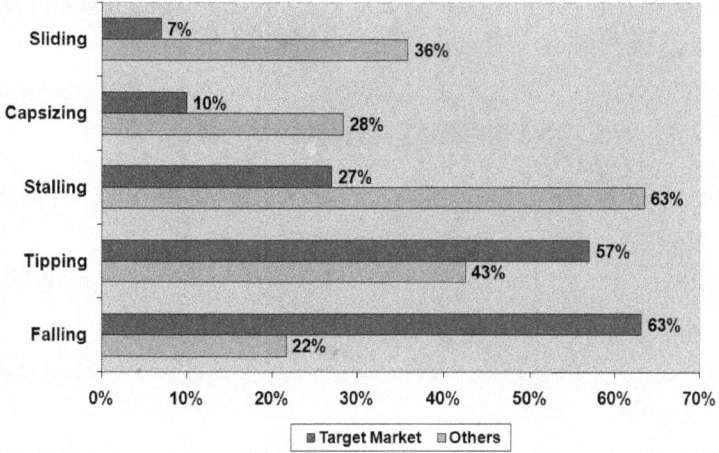

Chart 21. *Target market's problems.*

22: Target Market's Desires

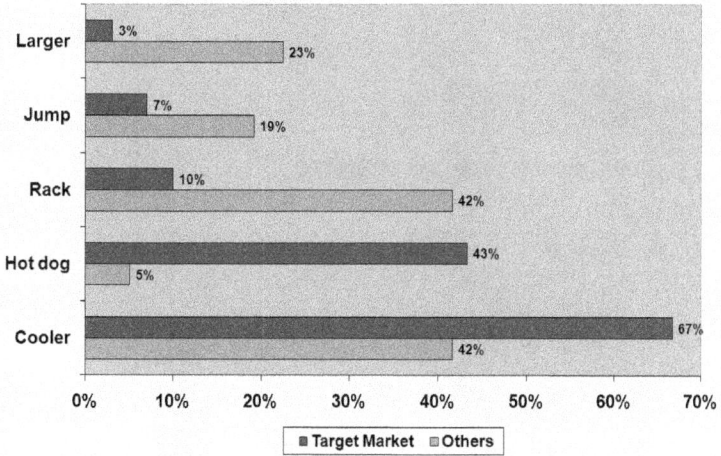

Chart 22. *Target market's desires.*

23: Target Market's Loyalty

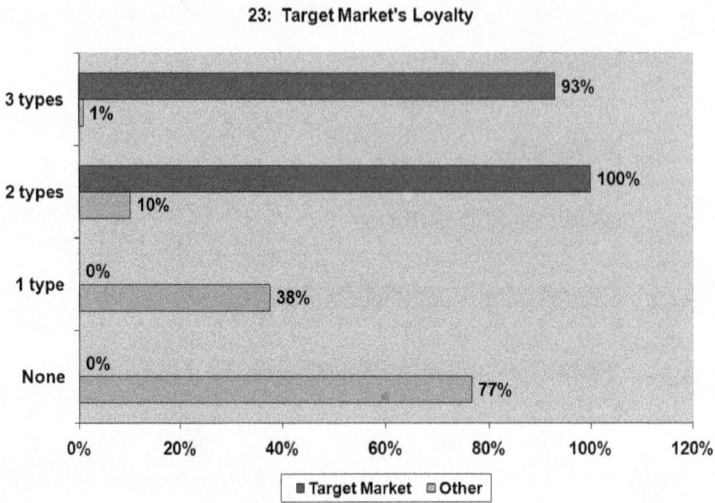

Chart 23. *Target market's loyalty.*

24: Target Market's Criteria

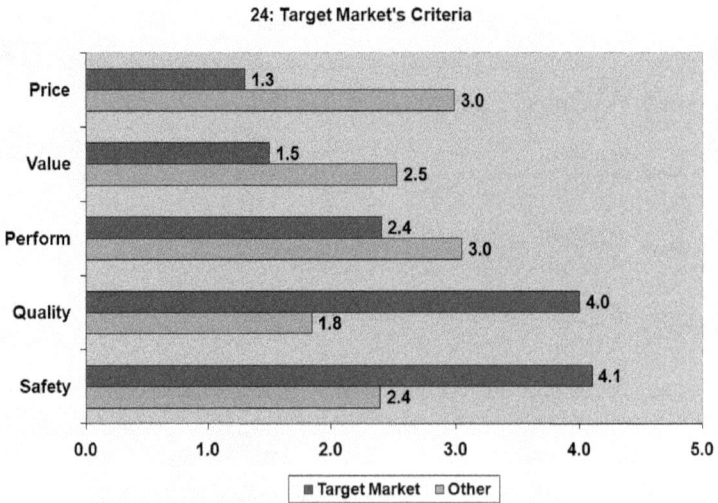

Chart 24. *Target market's criteria.*

25: Target Market's Usage

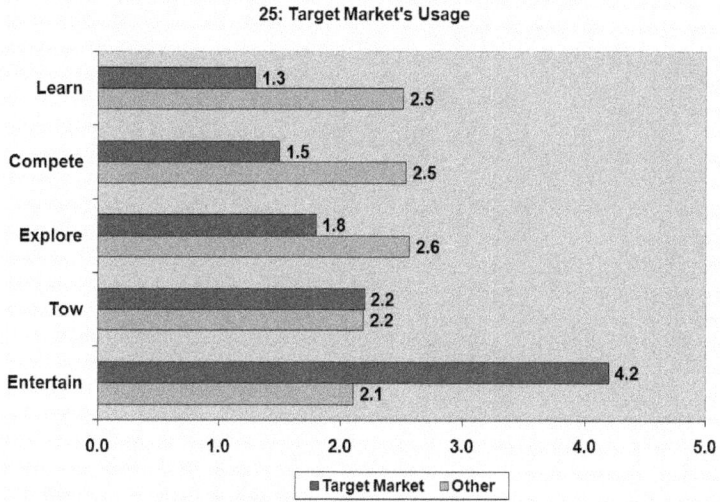

Chart 25. Target market's usage.

26: Target Market's Benefits

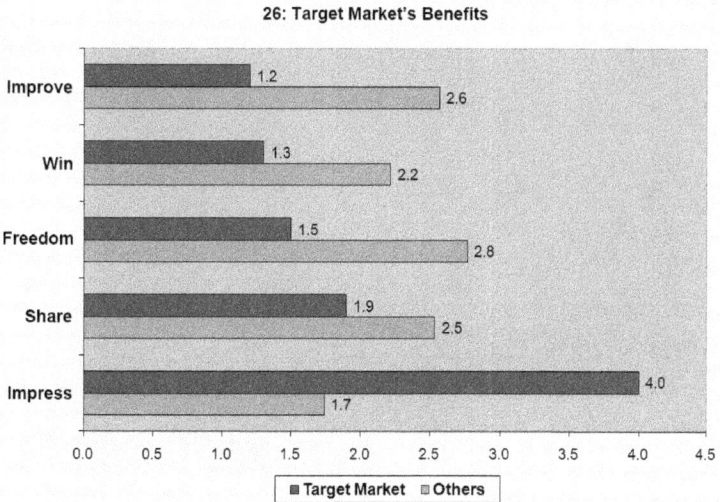

Chart 26. Target market's benefits.

APPENDIX 3

How to Analyze Overall Customers

A3.1 Code and Enter Customer Responses

Microsoft Excel sequentially assigns numbers to each row and assigns letters to each column of a worksheet. As shown in Appendix 6, the first column (ID) identifies the 150 respondents (A2–A151), while the first row sequentially labels all of the items in the survey (A1–BI1). In the second row, we entered the code numbers of the first respondent's responses in successive order (A2:BI2), and in each subsequent row we entered all the responses of the other respondents.

> We froze the first row and all proxy variables (A1–BI1). so we could continue to see the column headings as we scrolled through the data. We also pasted the column headings on an empty row below the data so we could analyze the data more easily.

A3.2 Count Responses and Purchases

After entering the data, we confirmed that all of the respondents answered each item of the survey. To do this, we highlighted A153:BI153 and entered "=COUNT(A2:BI151)" to make sure there were 150 responses for each item. We clicked on C154 and entered "=SUM(C2:C151)" to count the number of two-passenger models, while we clicked on D154 and entered "=SUM(D2:D151)" to count the number of three-passenger models.

> Data is missing if a column's count is less than the size of the sample.

A3.3 Confirm the Fulfillment of Quotas

We checked the quota for two-passenger models in column C by clicking on empty cell C156 and entering "=COUNTIF(C2:C151,1)" to count the number of respondents who owned one 2-passenger model and "=COUNTIF(C2:C151,2)" to count the number of respondents who owned two. We continued this process to confirm that the quotas were fulfilled for two-passenger models (column C), three-passenger models (column D), coastal owners (column E), and inland owners (column F).

A3.4 Calculate Percentages for Nonmetric Items

We calculated percentages for each nonmetric item by counting the positive responses and dividing by the sample size. To calculate the percentage for Item 1.1 in column F, we formated an empty cell by selecting "Format," "Number," and "Percentage," and entered "=COUNTIF(F2:F151,1)/150." We revised this formula to calculate the percentages for all nonmetric responses (items S-4, 1.1–3.3, and 12–14 in columns E–R and BG–BI).

A3.5 Calculate Averages for Metric Items

Our next step was to average metric responses by designating the range of cells to be averaged. To average the metric responses in column S, we formated an empty cell with one decimal place and entered "=AVERAGE(S2:S151)." We revised this formula to average all metric responses (items S-2, S-3, and 4.1–11.5 in columns C, D, and S–BF).

A3.6 Compile Tables for the Report

After analyzing the data, we pasted the results into the tables as shown in Appendix 6. After briefly naming each table and its rows in the first column, we entered the results in the second column.

A3.7 Pivot the Tables Into Bar Charts

We highlighted each table and selected "Insert," "Bar Chart," "Horizontal," and "New Page" to pivot each table into a bar chart. After labeling the chart and displaying its values, we clicked on the chart and chose "Format" and "Selected Chart Area" to change the font.

A3.8 Outline the Report

After outlining the report, we stated each survey question, and inserted the bar charts. To insert a bar chart, we entered "Select All," "Copy," "Paste," and "Paste Special," and pasted the chart into the report as a "Microsoft Office Excel Chart Object."

A3.9 Summarize the Results in Descending Order

We summarized the results in descending order, and inserted them after the relevant questions as shown in Appendix 1.

How to Segment Customers by Profitability

A4.1 Define the Loyalty Index as the Proxy for Potential Profit per Item

Items 3.1–3.3 in columns P–R elicit the customers' commitment to Jet-Spray models, a dealer, and equipment so we defined the loyalty index as the aggregate of these components of customer loyalty. To calculate the loyalty index score for the first respondent (row 2), we clicked on cell BJ2 and entered "=SUM(P2:R2)." We obtained the loyalty index score for other respondents by copying and pasting this formula to BJ3 through BJ151.

A4.2 Define Seating Capacity as the Proxy for Volume of Items

The survey of JetSpray customers (Figure 5) elicited the purchase volume of JetSprays with item S-2 (column C) for two-passenger models and item S-3 (column D) for three-passenger models. We defined seating capacity as two for each two-passenger model and as three for each three-passenger model. To calculate seating capacity for the first respondent, we clicked on cell BK2 and entered "=(C2*2)+(D2*3)." Then we calculated the seating capacity for the other respondents by copying and pasting this formula to BK3 through BK151.

A4.3 Define the Profitability Index as the Proxy for Profit From Customers

We defined the *profitability index* as seating capacity times the loyalty index and calculated the profitability index score for the first respondent by clicking on BL2 and entering "=BJ2*BK2." To obtain the profitability index scores for the other respondents, we pasted this formula to BL3 through BL151.

A4.4 Sort Respondents by Their Profitability Index Scores

Figure 6 sorts the 150 respondents in descending order by their profitability index score. We created Figure 6 by highlighting range BL2–BL151 and selecting "Data," "Sort," and "Column BL."

A4.5 Define the Profitability Segments

Table 14 reports in ascending order the profitability index scores of the respondents. We defined the top market segment as the 20% of the respondents who scored at least 10 on the profitability index. To create Table 14 we selected "Tools," "Data Analysis," and "Histogram"; specified BL2:BL151; and checked "Worksheet Ply." Then we edited the table with labels and added breakpoints for the market segments.

A4.6 Chart the Profitability Segments

We charted the respondents by their profitability by copying the profitability index scores to empty cells and selecting "Tools," "Data," "Analysis," "Histogram," and "Chart Output." Since "Bin" refers to the grouping interval for each bar, we highlighted all but the last profitability index score. Figure 7 shows how we added profitability segments to the bar chart.

A4.7 Create a Pie Chart of the Profitability Segments

The pie chart in Figure 8 depicts the market segments in Figure 7. To create this figure, we created a table in Excel with the percentage in each market segment, highlighted this table, and selected "Insert," "Chart," and "Pie." Then we edited the color saturation of each section to indicate the relative profitability of the market segments.

APPENDIX 5

How to Profile a Target Market

A5.1 Calculate Percentages for Nonmetric Items for Both Groups

Throughout the report on JetSpray's top market segment (Appendix 2), *target market* refers to the 30 respondents in the top market segment (i.e., rows 2–31), while *others* refers to the 120 other respondents (i.e., rows 32–151). To calculate percentages for item 1.1 in column F, we clicked on an empty cell; selected "Format," "Number," and "Percentage" and entered "=COUNTIF(F2:F31,1)/30" for the percentage of target market responses and entered "=COUNTIF(F32:F151,1)/120" for the percentage of other responses. We revised this formula to calculate the percentages of positive responses for both groups to all nonmetric questions (items S-4, 1.1–3.3, and 12–14 in columns E–R and BG–BI).

A5.2 Test Whether the Percentages for the Two Groups Are Significantly Different

With a significance level of 0.05 (z value = 0.96) and an average sample size of 75, the hurdle for a significance difference between the two groups is 11.3% (i.e., the square root of 0.96/75). Thus the responses of two groups are significantly different for an item when their percentages differ by at least 11.3%.

A5.3 Average Metric Responses for Both Groups

We averaged the responses to item 4.1 (column S) by formatting empty cells with one decimal place and entering "=AVERAGE(S2:S31)" for the target market and entering "=AVERAGE(S32:S151)" for the other respondents. We revised this formula to average responses for both groups to all metric questions (items S-2, S-3, and 4.1–11.5 in columns C, D, and S–BF).

A5.4 Test If the Averages Are Significantly Different for the Two Groups

The *t*-test of the difference between group means compares the averages of two groups and reports the probability that the averages are from the same population. If the probability (*p* value) is less than 0.05, the averages of the two groups are significantly different for the item. To test for a significant difference between group means, we selected "Tools," "Data Analysis," and "*T*-Test: Two Sample for Means," and entered the ranges for our two groups. For example, with item 4.1 (column S) the range was S2:S31 for the target market and S32:S151 for others.

A5.5 Compile Tables for the Report

After analyzing the data, we pasted the results into tables, as shown in Appendix 6. We briefly labeled each table and its rows in the first column, reported on others in the second column, and reported on the target market in the third column.

A5.6 Pivot the Tables Into Bar Charts

To pivot each table into a chart, we highlighted it and selected "Insert," "Bar Chart," "Horizontal," and "New Page." After labeling the chart and displaying its values, we clicked on the chart and selected "Format" and "Selected Chart Area" to edit the chart.

A5.7 Outline the Report and Insert the Bar Charts Into the Outline

After outlining the report and stating each question, we entered "Select All," "Copy," "Paste," and "Paste Special" to paste each chart in the report as a "Microsoft Office Excel Chart Object."

A5.8 Summarize the Results and Mark Significant Differences Between Groups

We summarized the results for each item in descending order, and marked significant differences between the target market and others with an asterisk (*).

A5.9 Compile These Distinctions as a Buyer Profile

Table 15 lists the significant differences between the top market segment and other customers as a buyer profile for a typical member of the target market.

APPENDIX 6

Data Worksheet in Microsoft Excel

Row Codes

Rows	Market Segments
2–31	Top market segment (target market)
32–151	Middle and bottom market segments (others)
32–89	Middle market segment
90–151	Bottom market segment

Column Codes

Survey Questions	Columns	Specifics
ID#	A	Respondent identification number
Screener-1 Current owner of a JetSpray personal watercraft?	B	Qualifies as a customer
Screener-2 Own a two-passenger JetSpray model?	C	Number purchased
Screener-3 Own a three-passenger JetSpray model?	D	Number purchased
Screener-4 Location?	E	1 = County with a coastline 2 = Inland county

Survey Questions	Columns	Specifics
1 Problems with your JetSpray?	F	1.1 Stalling engine
	G	1.2 Falling off
	H	1.3 Sliding in sharp turns
	I	1.4 Tipping with heavy passengers
	J	1.5 Capsizing
2 Improvements wanted?	K	2.1 Hot dog boat
	L	2.2 Garage storage rack
	M	2.3 Built-in cooler
	N	2.4 Floating boat jump
	O	2.5 Larger model for skiing and wake boarding
3 Loyal to JetSpray?	P	3.1 JetSpray models
	Q	3.2 A JetSpray dealer
	R	3.3 JetSpray equipment
4 Rate your uses of JetSprays	S	4.1 Compete in races
	T	4.2 Entertain guests
	U	4.3 Explore waterways with a passenger
	V	4.4 Learn to improve engine performance
	W	4.5 Tow skiers and wake boarders
5 Rate JetSpray's benefits	X	5.1 Feeling free
	Y	5.2 Impressing guests
	Z	5.3 Improving mechanical skills
	AA	5.4 Sharing activities with another
	AB	5.5 Winning races
6 Rate your shopping criteria	AC	6.1 Quality
	AD	6.2 Performance
	AE	6.3 Safety
	AF	6.4 Value
	AG	6.5 Price
7 Rate your personality	AH	7.1 Competitive
	AI	7.2 Extraverted
	AJ	7.3 Nurturing
	AK	7.4 Playful
	AL	7.5 Technical

Survey Questions	Columns	Specifics
8 Rate your activities	AM	8.1 Play with my family
	AN	8.2 Compete in extreme sports
	AO	8.3 Improve engine performance
	AP	8.4 Share adventures with another
	AQ	8.5 Socialize in groups
9 Rate your reputation	AR	9.1 Adventurer
	AS	9.2 Comedian
	AT	9.3 Competitor
	AU	9.4 Self-sufficiency
	AV	9.5 Social climber
10 Rate your values	AW	10.1 Freedom
	AX	10.2 Ingenuity
	AY	10.3 Nature
	AZ	10.4 Social status
	BA	10.5 Achievement
11 Rate your media use	BB	11.1 *Parade of Homes* magazine
	BC	11.2 *Popular Mechanics* magazine
	BD	11.3 Situation comedies on TV
	BE	11.4 Charts of local waterways
	BF	11.5 *Extreme Sports* magazine
12 Age level?	BG	1 = Under 30
		2 = 30s
		3 = 40s
		4 = 50s
		5 = 60 or older
13 Income level?	BH	1 = Struggler
		2 = Striver
		3 = Achiever
		4 = Wealthy
14 Gender?	BI	1 = Male
		2 = Female
Loyalty index	BJ	P + Q + R
Purchases	BK	(C x 2) + (D x 3)
Profitability index	BL	BJ x BK

Top Left Section (A1:U58)

Ro	A	B	C	D	E	F1	G1	H1	I1	J1	K2	L2	M2	N2	O2	P3	Q3	R3	S4	T4	U4
2	14	1	4	4	2	0	0	0	0	0	1	0	1	0	0	1	1	1	1	5	1
3	2	1	0	6	2	0	1	0	1	0	1	0	1	0	0	1	1	1	1	5	1
4	4	1	0	6	2	0	0	0	1	0	0	0	0	0	0	1	1	1	1	5	1
5	7	1	0	6	2	1	0	0	1	0	1	0	1	0	0	1	1	1	1	5	1
6	2	1	0	6	2	0	1	0	0	0	1	0	0	0	0	1	1	1	1	5	1
7	3	1	0	6	1	0	1	0	0	0	1	0	1	0	0	1	1	1	1	5	1
8	5	1	0	6	2	0	1	0	1	0	1	0	1	0	0	1	1	1	1	5	1
9	11	1	0	6	2	0	1	0	1	0	1	0	1	0	0	1	1	1	1	5	1
10	16	1	0	6	2	0	1	0	1	0	0	0	1	0	0	1	1	1	1	5	2
11	21	1	0	6	2	0	1	0	1	1	0	0	1	0	0	1	1	1	1	5	1
12	18	1	0	4	2	1	1	0	1	0	0	0	1	0	0	1	1	1	1	5	1
13	30	1	0	4	2	0	1	0	1	0	1	0	1	0	0	1	1	1	1	5	1
14	9	1	6	0	2	0	1	0	1	0	0	0	0	0	0	1	1	1	1	5	1
15	15	1	6	0	2	0	1	0	0	0	1	0	1	0	0	1	1	1	1	5	1
16	19	1	6	0	2	0	0	0	0	0	0	0	1	0	0	1	1	1	1	5	1
17	24	1	6	0	2	0	1	0	1	0	1	0	1	0	0	1	1	1	1	5	1
18	27	1	6	0	2	1	1	0	0	0	0	0	1	0	0	1	1	1	1	5	2
19	29	1	6	0	2	0	1	0	1	0	1	0	1	0	0	1	1	1	1	5	1
20	10	1	0	4	2	0	1	0	0	0	1	0	1	0	0	1	1	0	1	5	1
21	22	1	0	2	2	0	1	0	0	0	0	0	0	0	0	1	1	1	1	5	1
22	25	1	0	2	2	0	1	0	1	0	1	0	0	0	0	1	1	1	1	5	1
23	32	1	0	2	2	0	1	0	0	0	0	0	0	0	0	1	1	1	1	3	5
24	64	1	0	2	1	1	0	0	1	0	0	0	1	0	0	1	1	1	2	3	5
25	31	1	0	2	1	0	0	0	1	0	0	1	1	0	0	1	1	1	1	2	5
26	38	1	0	2	2	0	0	0	1	0	0	1	1	0	0	1	1	1	1	2	5
27	142	1	0	2	2	1	0	1	0	0	0	0	1	0	1	1	1	1	4	3	2
28	77	1	2	0	2	1	0	1	0	1	0	1	0	1	0	1	1	1	5	1	2
29	81	1	2	0	2	1	0	0	0	1	0	0	1	0	1	1	1	1	5	2	2
30	66	1	2	2	1	1	0	0	1	0	0	0	0	0	0	1	0	0	1	3	5
31	121	1	1	1	2	0	0	0	0	0	0	0	0	0	0	1	1	0	3	1	1
32	17	1	2	0	2	0	1	0	1	0	1	0	0	0	0	1	1	0	1	5	1
33	52	1	1	2	1	1	0	0	1	0	0	1	1	0	0	1	0	0	2	3	5
34	74	1	2	0	1	1	0	0	0	1	0	1	0	0	0	1	0	0	5	1	2
35	8	1	0	2	2	0	1	0	1	0	1	0	0	0	0	1	0	0	1	5	2
36	12	1	1	0	1	1	1	0	1	0	1	0	1	0	0	1	1	1	1	5	1
37	13	1	0	2	2	0	1	0	1	0	0	0	0	0	0	1	0	0	1	5	1
38	26	1	0	2	2	0	1	0	1	1	0	1	0	0	0	1	0	0	1	5	1
39	34	1	0	2	2	0	0	0	1	0	0	1	0	0	0	1	0	0	3	3	5
40	37	1	0	2	1	0	0	0	0	0	0	1	0	0	0	1	0	0	2	3	5
41	40	1	0	2	2	0	0	0	0	0	0	0	0	0	0	1	0	0	2	3	5
42	42	1	0	2	1	1	0	0	1	0	0	1	1	0	0	1	0	0	2	2	5
43	45	1	0	2	1	1	0	0	0	0	0	1	0	0	0	1	0	0	2	3	5
44	49	1	0	2	1	0	0	0	1	0	0	1	1	0	0	1	0	0	2	3	5
45	54	1	0	2	1	0	0	0	1	0	0	1	1	0	0	1	0	0	1	2	5
46	58	1	0	2	1	1	1	0	1	0	0	0	1	0	0	1	0	0	2	3	5
47	59	1	0	2	1	0	0	0	0	0	0	0	1	0	0	1	0	0	2	2	5
48	63	1	0	2	1	1	0	0	1	0	0	0	1	0	0	1	0	0	2	3	5
49	129	1	0	1	1	1	0	0	1	0	0	1	0	1	1	1	0	0	2	3	2
50	130	1	0	1	2	0	0	1	1	1	0	0	1	0	1	1	1	0	2	3	2
51	138	1	0	1	2	1	0	1	1	0	0	0	1	0	1	1	1	0	1	3	2
52	139	1	0	1	1	1	1	1	1	0	0	0	1	0	1	1	1	0	2	2	2
53	141	1	0	1	2	0	0	1	1	0	0	0	1	0	1	1	1	0	2	3	3
54	143	1	0	1	2	1	1	1	1	0	0	0	1	0	1	1	1	0	2	2	2
55	145	1	0	1	2	1	1	1	1	0	0	0	1	0	1	1	1	0	2	3	3
56	146	1	0	1	2	0	0	0	1	0	0	1	0	1	1	1	0	4	3	2
57	148	1	0	1	2	1	0	1	1	1	0	1	0	1	1	1	1	0	2	3	2
58	149	1	0	1	1	1	1	1	1	0	0	0	1	0	1	1	1	0	2	3	3

Note: A1:U58 defines the top left section of the data collected with the survey in Figure 5. The first row labels survey items, while the first column identifies respondents. (A1 refers to the ID label in the first row, while U58 refers to question 4, item 3, as rated by respondent 57.)

Middle Left Section (A59:U115)

Rc	A	B	C	D	E	F	G	H	I	J	K	L	M	N	O	P	Q	R	S	T	U
59	89	1	2	0	1	0	1	0	0	1	0	0	0	1	0	1	0	0	5	1	2
60	106	1	2	0	1	0	0	0	0	0	0	1	0	0	0	1	0	0	1	1	1
61	126	1	2	0	1	0	0	0	0	0	0	1	0	0	0	1	0	0	1	1	2
62	33	1	0	1	2	1	0	0	1	0	0	0	1	0	0	1	0	0	2	3	5
63	35	1	0	1	1	1	1	0	0	0	0	0	0	0	1	1	0	0	2	2	5
64	39	1	0	1	1	0	0	0	1	0	0	0	1	0	1	1	0	0	2	3	5
65	41	1	0	1	1	0	1	0	1	0	0	0	0	0	0	1	0	0	2	3	5
66	44	1	0	1	2	0	0	0	1	1	0	0	1	0	1	1	0	0	2	3	5
67	46	1	0	1	1	0	0	0	1	0	0	0	1	0	0	1	0	0	2	2	5
68	47	1	0	1	1	1	0	0	0	0	0	1	0	0	0	1	0	0	3	3	5
69	48	1	0	1	2	0	0	0	1	0	0	0	1	0	0	1	0	0	2	3	5
70	51	1	0	1	1	0	0	0	0	0	0	0	0	0	1	1	0	0	2	2	5
71	53	1	0	1	1	0	0	0	1	1	0	0	1	0	0	1	0	0	2	3	5
72	55	1	0	1	2	1	0	0	0	0	0	1	1	0	1	1	0	0	2	3	5
73	56	1	0	1	1	1	0	0	1	0	0	0	0	0	0	1	0	0	2	3	5
74	60	1	0	1	1	0	0	0	0	0	0	1	1	0	0	1	0	0	2	3	5
75	61	1	0	1	2	1	0	0	1	0	0	0	1	0	1	1	0	0	2	3	5
76	62	1	0	1	1	1	0	0	1	0	0	0	1	0	0	1	0	0	1	2	5
77	65	1	0	1	1	1	0	0	0	0	0	0	1	0	0	1	0	0	2	4	5
78	131	1	0	1	1	1	0	0	1	0	0	0	1	0	1	1	0	0	2	3	2
79	133	1	0	1	2	1	0	1	1	1	0	0	1	0	1	1	0	0	2	3	2
80	134	1	0	1	2	1	0	1	0	1	0	0	1	0	1	1	0	0	2	3	3
81	136	1	0	1	2	1	0	1	1	1	0	0	0	0	1	1	0	0	2	3	2
82	144	1	0	1	1	1	0	1	1	1	0	0	0	0	1	1	0	0	2	3	2
83	70	1	1	0	1	1	1	1	0	0	0	0	0	1	0	1	0	0	5	1	2
84	85	1	1	0	2	0	0	1	0	1	0	0	0	1	0	1	0	0	5	1	2
85	97	1	1	0	2	1	1	1	0	1	0	1	0	1	0	1	0	0	5	1	3
86	115	1	1	0	2	0	0	0	0	0	0	1	0	0	1	1	0	0	1	1	1
87	124	1	1	0	1	1	0	0	0	0	0	0	0	0	1	1	0	0	1	1	1
88	127	1	1	0	1	1	0	0	0	0	0	1	0	0	1	1	0	0	1	1	1
89	150	1	1	0	2	1	0	0	1	0	0	0	0	0	1	1	0	0	2	3	2
90	3	1	2	2	2	1	1	0	0	0	1	0	0	0	0	0	0	0	1	5	2
91	20	1	0	2	2	0	1	0	1	0	1	0	1	0	0	0	0	0	1	5	1
92	23	1	0	4	2	1	1	0	0	0	0	1	0	0	0	0	0	0	1	5	1
93	28	1	0	2	2	0	0	0	0	0	0	1	0	0	0	0	0	0	1	5	1
94	36	1	0	2	1	1	0	0	1	1	0	0	1	0	0	0	0	0	2	3	5
95	43	1	0	1	2	1	0	0	1	0	0	1	1	0	0	0	0	0	3	3	5
96	50	1	0	1	1	0	1	0	1	0	0	0	1	0	0	0	0	0	2	3	5
97	57	1	0	1	2	0	0	0	1	0	0	0	1	0	0	0	0	0	2	3	5
98	67	1	2	0	2	1	0	1	0	1	0	1	0	1	0	0	0	0	5	1	2
99	68	1	1	0	1	1	0	1	0	1	0	1	0	1	0	0	0	0	5	1	2
100	69	1	2	0	1	0	0	1	0	1	0	1	1	0	0	0	0	0	5	1	1
101	71	1	2	0	2	0	0	1	0	1	0	1	0	1	0	0	0	0	5	1	3
102	72	1	2	0	1	0	0	1	0	1	0	0	0	1	0	0	0	0	5	2	2
103	73	1	1	0	2	1	0	1	0	1	0	1	0	1	0	0	0	0	5	1	1
104	75	1	1	0	2	1	1	1	0	1	0	0	0	1	0	0	0	0	5	1	2
105	76	1	2	0	2	0	0	1	0	1	0	1	0	1	0	0	0	0	5	2	1
106	78	1	2	0	2	1	0	1	0	1	0	1	0	1	0	0	0	0	5	1	2
107	79	1	1	0	1	0	0	1	0	1	0	0	0	1	0	0	0	0	5	1	2
108	80	1	1	0	2	0	0	1	0	0	0	1	0	0	0	0	0	0	5	1	3
109	82	1	2	0	2	1	1	1	0	1	0	0	0	1	0	0	0	0	5	1	2
110	83	1	2	0	2	0	0	1	1	1	0	0	1	1	0	0	0	0	5	1	3
111	84	1	2	0	1	1	0	1	0	1	0	1	0	1	0	0	0	0	5	1	2
112	86	1	1	0	2	1	0	1	0	1	0	0	0	0	0	0	0	0	5	1	2
113	87	1	2	0	2	1	1	1	0	0	0	1	0	1	0	0	0	0	5	2	1
114	88	1	2	0	2	1	0	1	0	1	0	1	0	1	0	0	0	0	5	1	2
115	90	1	1	0	2	1	0	1	0	1	0	1	0	0	0	0	0	0	5	1	2

Note: A59:U115 defines the middle left section of the survey data. (A59 refers to the ID of respondent 58, while U115 refers to question 4, item 3, as rated by respondent 114.)

Bottom Left Section (A116:U170)

Ro	A	B	C	D	E	F	G	H	I	J	K	L	M	N	O	P	Q	R	S	T	U
	A1	B5	C5	D5	E5	F1	G1	H1	I1	J1	K2	L2	M2	N2	O2	P3	Q3	R3	S4	T4	U4
116	91	1	2	0	2	1	0	1	0	1	0	1	0	0	0	0	0	0	5	1	1
117	92	1	2	0	2	0	0	1	1	1	0	1	1	0	0	0	0	0	5	1	2
118	93	1	1	0	2	1	0	1	0	0	0	0	1	0	1	0	0	0	5	1	2
119	94	1	2	0	2	1	1	1	0	1	0	0	0	1	0	0	0	0	5	2	2
120	95	1	2	0	2	0	0	1	0	1	0	1	0	1	0	0	0	0	5	1	2
121	96	1	2	0	2	1	0	0	0	1	0	1	0	0	0	0	0	0	5	1	2
122	98	1	2	0	2	0	0	1	0	0	0	1	1	1	0	0	0	0	5	1	2
123	99	1	1	0	1	1	0	0	0	0	0	1	0	0	0	0	0	0	3	1	1
124	100	1	1	0	1	1	0	0	0	0	0	1	0	0	0	0	0	0	2	1	1
125	101	1	1	0	1	1	0	0	0	0	0	1	0	0	0	0	0	0	1	1	1
126	102	1	2	0	2	0	0	0	0	0	0	0	0	0	0	0	0	0	3	1	2
127	103	1	1	0	2	1	0	0	0	0	0	1	0	0	0	0	0	0	1	1	1
128	104	1	1	1	2	1	0	0	0	0	0	0	0	0	0	0	0	0	2	1	1
129	105	1	1	0	1	1	0	0	0	0	0	1	0	0	0	0	0	0	1	1	1
130	107	1	1	0	0	1	0	0	0	0	0	1	0	0	0	0	0	0	1	1	1
131	108	1	2	0	2	1	0	0	0	0	0	0	0	0	0	0	0	0	1	1	2
132	109	1	1	0	1	0	0	0	0	0	0	1	0	0	0	0	0	0	1	1	1
133	110	1	2	0	1	1	0	0	0	0	0	0	0	0	0	0	0	0	2	1	1
134	111	1	1	1	2	1	0	0	0	0	0	1	0	0	0	0	0	0	1	1	1
135	112	1	1	0	1	1	0	0	0	0	0	0	0	0	0	0	0	0	1	1	1
136	113	1	2	0	1	0	0	0	0	0	0	0	0	0	0	0	0	0	1	1	1
137	114	1	2	0	2	1	0	0	0	0	0	1	0	0	0	0	0	0	1	1	2
138	116	1	1	1	2	1	0	0	0	0	0	0	0	0	0	0	0	0	2	1	1
139	117	1	1	0	1	1	0	0	0	0	0	0	0	0	0	0	0	0	1	1	1
140	118	1	1	0	1	1	0	0	0	0	0	0	0	0	0	0	0	0	1	1	1
141	119	1	2	0	1	1	0	0	0	0	0	0	0	0	0	0	0	0	1	1	2
142	120	1	1	0	1	1	0	0	0	0	0	1	0	0	0	0	0	0	3	1	1
143	122	1	2	0	1	1	0	0	0	0	0	0	0	0	0	0	0	0	1	1	1
144	123	1	2	0	1	1	0	0	0	0	0	1	0	0	0	0	0	0	1	1	1
145	125	1	2	1	1	1	0	0	0	0	0	0	0	0	0	0	0	0	1	1	1
146	128	1	1	1	2	1	0	0	0	0	0	0	0	0	0	0	0	0	1	1	1
147	132	1	0	1	2	0	1	1	0	0	0	0	0	1	0	0	0	0	4	2	3
148	135	1	0	1	2	1	1	1	1	0	0	0	0	1	0	1	0	0	1	2	2
149	137	1	0	1	2	0	0	1	1	0	0	0	1	0	0	0	0	0	2	3	3
150	140	1	0	1	2	1	0	0	1	1	0	0	0	1	0	0	0	0	2	3	2
151	147	1	0	1	2	1	0	1	1	0	0	0	1	0	1	0	0	0	2	2	2
152	ID	S1	S2	S3	S4	1.1	1.2	1.3	1.4	1.5	2.1	2.2	2.3	2.4	2.5	3.1	3.2	3.3	4.1	4.2	4.3
153	Count	150	150	150	150	150	150	150	150	150	150	150	150	150	150	150	150	150	150	150	150
154	Sum	314	143	171		84	45	45	68	37	19	53	70	25	28	88	42	28	SUM		
155	Mean	2.09	46%	54%														MEAN 2.3		2.5	2.4

		2-Seat	3-Seat		Count	Counts	56%	30%	30%	45%	25%	13%	35%	47%	17%	19%	59%	28%	19% percent
156	Count	2-Seat	3-Seat	Count	Counts	56%	30%	30%	45%	25%	13%	35%	47%	17%	19%	59%	28%	19% percent	
157	0	76	65	Coast:	60	Problem		Desire											Usage Mean
158	1	33	45	Inland	90	Stallin 56%		Coole 47%		Count Loyalty		Logal		Entert 2.5					
159	2	35	26		150	Tippin 45%		Rack 35%		62	None 41%		Model 53%		Explor 2.4				
160	4	1	5	Quota 40%		Falling 30%		Large 19%		46	1 type 31%		Dealer 28%		Comp 2.3				
161	6	6	9	Quota 60%		Sliding 30%		Jump 17%		14	2 type 9%		Equip 19%		Learn 2.3				
162	Count	75	85			Capsi 25%		Hot d 13%		28	3 type 19%			Tov 2.2					
163	50%	50%	7% bot	Count	Others	Target Proble	Others	Target Mark	Desire	Other	Target Marke	Logal	Other	Target Market					
164		2-Seat	3-Seat	Coasta 0	0	Falling 22%	63%	Coole 42%	67%	None 77%	0%	Use Other							
165	0	50%	43%	Inland 1	1	Tippin 43%	57%	Hot d 5%	43%	1 type 38%	0%	Entert 2.1							
166	1	22%	30%			Stallin 63%	27%	Rack 42%	10%	2 type 10%	100%	Tov 2.2							
167	2	23%	17%			Capsi 28%	10%	Jump 19%	7%	3 type 1%	93%	Explor 2.6							
168	4	1%	3%			Sliding 36%	7%	Larger 23%	3%			Comp 2.5							
169	6	4%	6%	2-p	3-p		2-p	3-p	Target Other	T	Other	Learn 2.5							
170		100%	100%	Target 47%	87%	Others 36%	84%	no 2p 19%	56%	no 3p 80%	57%								

Note: A116:U170 defines the bottom left section of the survey data. (A116 refers to the ID of respondent 115, while U170 refers to the bottom right of the relevant analysis.)

Top Center Section (V1:AQ58)

Re	V4	V4	X5	Y5	Z5	AA	AB	AC	AD	AE	AF	AG	AH	AI	AJ	AK	AL	AM	AN	AO	AP	AQ
2	1	3	1	5	1	1	1	5	2	5	1	1	3	5	2	2	1	1	1	1	3	5
3	1	2	1	5	1	1	1	4	2	5	1	1	3	5	2	3	1	3	1	1	4	5
4	1	3	1	5	1	1	1	5	3	5	1	1	3	5	2	1	1	3	1	1	3	5
5	1	2	1	5	1	1	1	5	2	5	1	1	1	5	2	2	1	1	1	1	3	5
6	1	2	1	5	1	1	1	5	2	5	1	1	3	5	2	2	1	1	1	1	3	5
7	1	2	1	5	1	2	1	4	2	5	1	1	1	5	2	3	1	4	1	1	3	5
8	1	2	1	5	1	1	1	5	2	5	1	1	2	5	2	1	1	1	1	1	4	5
9	1	2	1	5	1	1	1	5	2	5	1	1	3	5	2	1	1	1	1	1	3	5
10	1	2	1	5	1	1	1	4	2	5	1	1	3	5	2	1	1	3	1	1	2	4
11	1	2	1	5	1	1	1	5	2	5	1	1	3	5	2	1	1	2	1	1	2	5
12	1	2	1	5	1	1	1	5	3	5	1	1	3	5	2	3	1	4	1	1	3	5
13	1	2	1	5	1	1	1	5	2	5	1	1	1	5	2	2	1	1	1	1	3	5
14	1	3	1	5	1	1	1	5	1	5	1	1	2	5	2	3	1	1	1	1	3	4
15	1	2	1	5	1	2	1	5	2	5	1	1	1	5	2	2	1	1	1	1	3	5
16	1	3	1	5	1	1	1	5	2	5	1	1	3	5	2	2	1	3	1	1	3	5
17	1	2	1	5	1	1	1	5	2	5	1	1	3	5	2	2	1	2	1	1	3	5
18	1	3	1	5	1	1	1	4	1	5	1	1	2	5	2	1	1	1	1	1	3	5
19	1	2	1	5	1	1	1	5	2	5	1	1	1	5	2	2	1	1	1	1	3	5
20	1	2	1	5	1	1	1	5	2	5	1	1	1	5	2	2	1	2	1	1	2	5
21	1	2	1	5	1	2	1	5	3	5	1	1	3	5	2	3	1	1	1	1	3	5
22	1	2	1	5	1	1	1	5	2	5	1	1	1	5	2	2	1	1	1	1	3	5
23	1	2	1	5	1	2	1	3	3	5	4	1	3	3	2	3	1	1	1	1	3	3
24	1	2	3	2	1	5	1	3	3	2	4	1	3	2	4	3	1	3	1	1	5	1
25	1	2	2	1	1	5	1	2	3	1	2	2	2	3	4	2	1	3	1	1	4	2
26	1	2	2	1	1	5	1	2	3	1	2	2	2	3	4	2	2	3	1	1	5	3
27	2	5	4	2	2	4	1	1	3	2	4	5	2	3	1	4	3	3	3	2	3	1
28	2	2	5	1	2	3	5	3	5	1	1	1	5	1	1	3	4	1	5	2	1	3
29	3	1	5	1	1	3	5	1	5	1	1	1	5	1	1	3	2	1	5	1	1	3
30	1	1	2	2	2	5	1	2	3	3	3	1	1	3	3	2	1	2	1	1	5	2
31	5	1	1	1	4	1	1	1	1	2	4	2	1	1	2	5	2	1	5	1	1	1
32	1	2	1	5	1	1	1	5	2	5	1	1	1	5	2	2	1	1	1	1	3	5
33	1	2	2	2	1	5	1	2	2	4	2	1	3	3	4	2	2	3	1	1	5	2
34	2	3	5	1	2	1	5	3	5	1	2	1	5	1	1	4	2	1	5	2	1	2
35	1	2	1	5	1	1	1	5	2	5	1	1	2	5	2	2	1	3	1	1	2	5
36	1	2	1	5	1	1	1	4	3	5	1	1	3	5	2	1	1	1	1	1	3	5
37	1	2	1	5	1	1	1	5	2	5	1	1	2	5	2	1	1	2	1	1	4	5
38	1	2	1	5	1	2	1	5	2	5	1	1	2	5	2	2	1	4	1	1	4	5
39	1	2	2	1	1	5	1	2	3	3	4	2	2	3	4	2	1	4	1	1	5	2
40	1	2	2	1	1	5	1	3	2	4	2	2	3	3	5	2	1	3	1	1	4	4
41	1	2	2	1	1	5	1	3	2	4	2	1	2	3	5	2	1	3	1	1	4	4
42	1	3	2	1	1	5	2	2	3	4	2	1	2	3	4	2	2	3	1	1	5	3
43	1	2	3	1	1	5	1	3	2	4	5	2	2	3	4	2	1	3	1	1	4	3
44	1	2	3	1	2	5	1	2	3	4	2	2	2	2	4	2	1	3	1	1	4	3
45	1	2	2	1	2	5	1	2	3	4	2	1	1	3	4	1	1	3	1	1	5	2
46	1	3	2	2	1	5	1	3	3	2	3	1	2	3	4	1	3	1	1	1	5	2
47	1	3	2	1	2	5	1	2	3	4	4	2	2	4	5	2	1	4	1	1	5	2
48	1	2	2	1	2	5	1	2	3	4	1	3	2	3	5	1	1	3	1	1	5	2
49	2	5	4	2	2	2	2	1	2	2	3	5	2	3	2	2	2	4	2	2	4	1
50	2	5	3	2	3	4	2	1	3	4	3	4	3	4	2	5	2	5	3	2	3	1
51	3	5	4	2	2	2	1	1	2	4	3	5	2	4	1	3	2	3	3	2	4	2
52	2	5	4	2	3	4	1	1	4	5	3	4	3	3	2	4	4	1	3	1	3	1
53	3	5	4	3	2	3	1	1	2	2	3	5	3	4	2	5	1	3	2	3	4	2
54	2	5	4	3	2	3	2	1	4	4	3	5	4	3	2	4	2	5	4	2	4	1
55	3	5	4	2	2	2	1	1	2	4	4	5	4	4	2	4	2	4	2	2	3	1
56	2	5	5	2	2	4	2	1	4	2	3	5	2	3	2	5	3	3	3	2	4	2
57	2	5	4	2	2	3	1	1	4	3	4	4	4	3	2	4	2	3	2	4	4	1
58	3	5	5	3	2	4	2	1	3	4	3	5	3	4	2	5	3	3	2	1	5	2

Note: V1:AQ58 defines the top center section of the survey data. (V1 refers to the label for question 4, item 4, while AQ58 refers to question 8, item 5, as rated by respondent 57.)

Middle Center Section (V59:AQ115)

Row	V4	V4	X5	Y5	Z5	AA	AB	AC	AD	AE	AF	AG	AH	AI	AJ	AK	AL	AM	AN	AO	AP	AQ
59	1	3	3	1	1	1	5	3	5	1	3	1	5	1	1	3	2	1	5	1	1	2
60	5	1	2	1	5	1	1	1	2	1	2	5	2	1	1	2	5	1	1	5	2	1
61	5	1	2	1	5	1	1	1	2	1	2	5	1	1	1	2	5	3	1	5	1	1
62	1	2	2	1	2	5	1	2	3	3	5	1	2	3	5	2	2	3	1	1	4	2
63	1	3	3	2	2	5	2	3	2	4	4	3	1	3	4	1	1	2	1	1	4	3
64	1	1	2	2	2	5	1	3	3	4	4	3	4	3	4	1	1	2	1	1	5	3
65	1	2	1	4	1	5	1	2	3	2	3	2	1	3	4	3	1	4	1	1	4	2
66	1	2	4	3	2	5	1	2	3	3	2	1	3	2	4	3	1	2	1	1	4	2
67	1	1	2	1	2	5	2	2	3	1	2	1	2	2	5	2	1	4	1	1	5	4
68	1	2	2	4	1	5	1	2	2	4	4	2	1	3	5	2	2	3	1	1	5	2
69	1	2	4	1	2	5	1	2	3	3	2	1	2	3	4	1	1	3	1	1	4	4
70	1	2	3	1	1	5	2	2	3	3	3	1	2	3	5	3	1	4	1	1	4	2
71	1	1	1	1	2	5	1	3	3	1	2	3	2	4	4	2	1	2	1	1	4	4
72	1	2	4	2	1	5	1	2	3	2	2	1	2	2	5	2	1	4	1	1	5	3
73	1	1	2	1	2	5	1	2	2	4	3	3	2	3	4	2	1	2	1	1	4	2
74	1	2	2	1	1	5	1	2	2	4	4	1	1	3	5	2	1	3	1	1	4	2
75	1	2	2	2	2	5	1	2	3	4	2	2	2	2	4	2	1	3	1	1	5	1
76	1	1	4	1	2	5	1	2	3	1	3	1	3	3	4	2	2	4	1	1	4	2
77	1	2	2	1	1	5	2	2	2	4	2	2	2	3	4	2	1	4	1	1	5	2
78	2	5	5	2	2	1	1	2	5	4	5	2	3	2	4	2	3	2	2	2	5	2
79	2	5	5	2	3	2	1	1	4	3	4	5	3	3	2	5	2	3	3	2	3	1
80	3	5	4	3	2	4	2	1	3	4	3	5	4	3	2	3	1	4	2	2	4	1
81	2	5	5	2	3	3	1	1	4	4	3	4	3	3	2	4	3	3	4	2	4	1
82	2	5	5	3	3	2	1	2	3	4	4	3	3	1	3	1	3	2	1	5	1	
83	3	1	5	1	3	3	5	2	5	2	1	1	5	1	1	4	2	1	5	2	2	3
84	2	1	5	1	2	1	5	2	5	1	1	3	4	1	1	3	4	1	5	2	2	2
85	2	3	3	1	2	1	5	2	4	1	2	1	5	1	1	4	2	1	5	2	1	3
86	5	1	1	1	4	2	1	1	2	1	2	5	2	1	1	2	5	2	1	5	1	1
87	4	1	1	1	5	1	2	1	2	1	2	5	2	1	1	3	5	2	1	5	1	1
88	5	1	2	1	5	1	2	1	3	1	2	5	2	1	1	2	5	1	1	5	1	1
89	2	5	4	2	2	2	1	2	3	3	5	1	2	3	1	1	4	2	1	4	1	
90	1	2	1	5	1	2	1	5	2	5	1	1	1	5	2	3	1	1	1	1	3	4
91	1	2	1	5	1	1	1	4	2	5	1	1	2	5	2	2	1	1	1	1	4	5
92	1	2	1	5	1	1	1	5	2	5	1	1	1	5	2	2	1	1	1	1	3	4
93	1	2	1	5	1	1	1	5	2	5	1	1	5	2	2	1	3	1	1	1	4	
94	1	2	2	1	1	5	1	2	2	3	3	1	2	4	5	2	1	3	1	1	4	2
95	1	2	2	1	2	5	1	2	3	4	4	1	2	3	5	2	1	3	1	1	5	2
96	1	3	2	3	1	5	1	2	2	4	3	2	3	3	4	2	1	3	1	1	5	2
97	1	2	1	1	1	5	1	2	3	4	2	1	3	2	2	3	1	1	1	4	2	
98	4	1	3	1	2	1	5	2	5	1	2	1	5	1	1	3	2	1	5	2	1	3
99	4	1	4	2	2	2	5	3	5	1	2	1	5	2	1	3	2	1	5	2	1	1
100	4	2	5	1	2	1	5	1	4	1	3	3	5	1	1	3	3	1	5	1	1	2
101	4	3	3	1	2	1	5	2	5	1	2	4	5	1	1	3	2	1	5	1	1	1
102	3	1	5	2	1	2	5	2	5	1	3	1	4	2	1	3	4	1	5	2	1	2
103	3	2	2	1	2	1	5	1	5	2	2	3	5	1	1	3	2	1	5	1	1	3
104	3	2	3	2	3	3	5	1	5	1	3	2	5	1	1	3	3	1	5	2	2	3
105	2	1	5	1	2	1	5	2	4	2	2	1	5	1	1	3	2	1	5	1	1	2
106	1	1	3	2	3	1	5	1	5	1	2	4	4	1	1	4	2	1	5	1	1	1
107	2	1	5	1	2	2	5	2	5	1	3	1	5	2	1	3	1	1	5	2	1	3
108	1	3	3	1	2	1	5	2	5	1	2	2	5	1	1	3	2	1	5	2	1	2
109	1	1	4	2	2	1	5	2	5	2	2	1	5	1	1	3	1	1	5	2	1	1
110	3	1	3	1	3	2	5	2	4	1	2	4	5	1	1	3	2	1	5	2	1	2
111	1	2	3	1	2	1	5	3	5	1	2	1	5	1	1	4	2	1	5	3	1	3
112	2	3	4	1	3	4	5	2	5	1	2	1	5	1	1	3	2	1	5	2	1	3
113	4	1	5	1	2	1	5	1	4	1	2	4	5	2	1	3	2	1	5	1	1	3
114	3	1	4	2	2	3	5	2	5	2	2	1	5	1	1	3	2	1	5	2	1	3
115	3	1	3	1	2	1	5	2	5	1	2	2	5	1	1	3	2	1	5	2	1	3

Note: V59:AQ115 defines the middle center section of the survey data. (V59 refers to question 4, item 4, as rated by respondent 58, while AQ115 refers to question 8, item 5, as rated by respondent 114.)

Bottom Center Section (V116:AQ169)

Re	V4	V4	X5	Y5	Z5	AA	AB	AC	AD	AE	AF	AG	AH	AI	AJ	AK	AL	AM	AN	AO	AP	AQ
116	1	1	4	1	2	3	5	2	5	1	2	1	5	1	1	4	3	1	5	2	1	1
117	1	2	3	1	2	1	5	2	4	1	1	1	5	1	1	3	2	1	5	1	1	3
118	2	1	5	1	3	1	5	3	5	1	2	4	4	2	1	3	2	1	5	2	1	2
119	2	1	3	2	2	1	5	2	5	1	2	1	5	1	1	4	1	1	5	2	1	3
120	1	3	4	1	1	2	5	2	5	1	2	1	5	1	1	3	2	1	5	1	1	1
121	3	1	3	1	2	1	5	1	5	2	3	4	5	1	1	3	4	1	5	2	1	2
122	2	1	3	2	1	1	5	2	5	1	2	2	5	1	1	3	2	1	5	2	1	3
123	5	1	2	1	5	1	1	1	2	1	2	5	2	1	1	2	5	1	1	5	1	1
124	5	1	2	1	5	1	1	1	2	1	3	5	1	1	1	3	5	2	1	5	1	1
125	5	1	2	1	5	2	1	1	2	1	2	5	2	1	1	2	4	1	1	5	1	1
126	5	1	1	1	5	1	1	1	2	1	2	4	2	1	2	2	5	2	1	5	2	1
127	5	1	1	1	4	1	1	1	1	1	4	5	2	1	1	3	5	1	1	5	1	1
128	5	1	1	1	5	1	1	1	2	1	2	5	2	1	1	2	4	1	1	5	1	1
129	5	1	2	1	5	1	1	1	2	1	2	5	1	1	1	2	5	2	1	5	1	1
130	5	1	2	1	5	1	1	1	2	1	3	5	2	1	1	2	5	3	1	5	1	1
131	5	1	1	1	4	2	2	1	3	1	2	5	2	1	2	2	5	1	1	5	1	1
132	5	1	2	1	5	1	1	1	2	1	2	5	2	1	1	3	5	1	1	5	1	1
133	5	1	1	1	5	1	1	1	2	1	4	4	2	1	1	2	4	2	1	5	1	1
134	5	1	1	1	5	1	1	1	2	1	2	5	1	1	1	2	5	1	1	5	1	1
135	5	1	2	1	5	1	1	1	1	1	2	5	2	1	1	2	5	1	1	5	2	1
136	5	1	2	1	5	1	6	1	2	1	3	5	2	1	1	2	5	2	1	5	1	1
137	5	1	2	1	5	1	1	1	2	1	2	5	2	1	1	3	5	1	1	5	2	1
138	5	1	2	1	5	1	1	1	3	1	3	4	2	1	1	2	4	1	1	5	1	1
139	5	1	2	1	5	1	1	1	2	1	2	5	1	1	1	2	4	3	1	5	1	1
140	5	1	2	1	5	1	2	1	2	1	2	5	2	1	1	3	5	1	1	5	1	1
141	5	1	2	1	5	1	1	1	2	1	4	5	2	1	2	2	5	2	1	5	1	1
142	5	1	2	1	5	1	1	1	2	1	2	5	2	1	1	2	5	1	1	5	2	1
143	5	1	2	1	5	2	1	1	2	1	3	5	2	1	1	2	4	1	1	5	1	1
144	5	1	2	1	5	1	1	1	2	1	2	5	2	1	1	2	5	1	1	5	1	1
145	5	1	2	1	5	1	1	1	2	1	3	5	2	1	2	2	5	1	1	5	2	1
146	5	1	1	1	4	1	1	1	2	1	2	5	2	1	1	2	4	1	1	5	1	1
147	3	5	4	3	2	3	2	1	3	4	3	4	4	4	1	4	3	4	4	1	3	1
148	2	5	4	2	2	1	1	3	2	4	4	5	2	5	3	1	4	2				
149	2	5	4	3	2	3	2	1	3	3	4	5	4	3	2	5	1	4	2	2	3	1
150	2	5	5	2	2	2	1	3	4	4	5	4	3	2	4	5	2	2	5	1		
151	2	5	4	3	3	2	2	1	2	5	3	5	2	3	1	4	1	5	4	1	5	1
152	4.4	4.5	5.1	5.2	5.3	5.4	5.5	6.1	6.2	6.3	6.4	6.5	7.1	7.2	7.3	7.4	7.5	8.1	8.2	8.3	8.4	8.5
153	0	0	0	0	0	0	0	0	0	0	0	0	0	0	0	0	0	0	0	0	0	0
154																						
155	2.3	2.2	2.5	2.2	2.3	2.4	2.0	2.3	2.9	2.7	2.3	2.6	2.7	2.6	2.1	2.6	2.2	2.2	2.1	2.1	2.7	2.5

156					
157	BeneMean	CriteMean	PersMean	LoveMean	FrienMean
158	Feel 2.5	Perf 2.9	Com 2.8	Shar 2.7	Self- 2.6
159	Shar 2.4	Safe 2.7	Extra 2.6	Soci 2.5	Com 2.5
160	Impr 2.3	Pric 2.7	Plas 2.6	Fami 2.2	Adve 2.2
161	Impr 2.2	Valu 2.3	Tech 2.2	Spor 2.1	Soci 2.0
162	Win 2.0	Quali 2.3	Nurt 2.1	Impr 2.1	Com 1.8
163					

164	Target Ma	Bene Othe	Target Ma	Crite Othe	Target Ma	Pers Othe	Target Ma	Love Othe	Target Ma	Frien Othe	Target Mar
165	4.2	Impr 1.7	4.0	Safe 2.4	4.1	Extra 2.2	4.2	Soci 2.1	4.1	Soci 1.5	3.8
166	2.2	Shar 2.5	1.9	Quali 1.8	4.0	Com 2.8	2.4	Shar 2.7	3.0	Com 2.6	2.3
167	1.8	Free 2.8	1.5	Perf 3.0	2.4	Plas 2.7	2.2	Fami 2.2	1.9	Self- 2.8	1.9
168	1.5	Win 2.2	1.3	Valu 2.5	1.5	Nurt 2.1	2.1	Impr 2.3	1.2	Adve 2.6	1.7
169	1.3	Impr 2.6	1.2	Pric 3.0	1.3	Tech 2.4	1.4	Spor 2.3	1.3	Com 2.8	1.3

Note: V116:AQ169 defines the bottom center section of the survey data. (V116 refers to question 4, item 4, as rated by respondent 115, while AQ169 refers to the bottom right of the relevant analysis.)

Top Right Section (AR1:BL58)

Ro	AR	AS	AT	AU	AV	AW	AX	AY	AZ	BA	BB	BC	BD	BE	BF	BG	BH	BI	BJ Lo	BK Se	BL Pr
2	1	1	1	2	5	1	1	3	4	2	4	1	4	1	1	4	4	1	3	20	60
3	1	1	2	2	5	2	1	2	4	2	4	1	3	1	1	5	4	1	3	18	54
4	1	1	2	2	5	2	1	2	5	2	5	1	4	1	1	5	4	2	3	18	54
5	1	1	2	2	5	2	1	1	4	2	5	1	4	1	1	5	4	2	3	18	54
6	1	1	2	2	5	1	1	2	5	2	5	1	4	1	1	4	3	2	3	18	54
7	1	1	2	1	5	1	1	2	5	3	5	1	4	1	1	4	4	1	3	18	54
8	1	1	2	2	5	1	1	1	5	2	5	1	5	1	1	4	4	2	3	18	54
9	1	1	2	1	5	2	1	2	5	2	5	1	4	1	1	3	4	2	3	18	54
10	1	2	2	2	5	1	1	2	5	2	5	1	4	1	1	4	3	2	3	18	54
11	1	1	3	2	5	1	1	3	4	3	5	1	4	1	1	5	4	2	3	18	54
12	1	1	2	2	5	1	1	1	5	2	3	1	5	1	1	4	4	2	3	12	36
13	1	1	4	2	5	1	1	1	5	2	5	1	4	1	1	4	4	2	3	12	36
14	1	1	3	2	5	1	1	2	5	4	5	1	4	1	1	4	3	2	3	12	36
15	1	1	2	1	5	1	1	1	5	2	5	1	4	1	1	5	4	2	3	12	36
16	1	1	3	2	5	1	1	3	5	2	5	1	4	1	1	4	3	2	3	12	36
17	1	2	2	1	5	2	1	1	5	2	5	1	4	1	1	4	4	2	3	12	36
18	1	1	2	2	3	1	1	1	4	2	5	1	4	1	1	5	4	2	3	12	36
19	1	1	4	2	5	1	1	2	5	2	5	1	4	1	1	4	4	2	3	12	36
20	1	1	2	2	5	1	1	3	5	2	5	1	3	1	1	4	4	2	2	12	24
21	1	1	2	2	4	1	1	1	5	2	4	1	4	1	1	4	3	2	3	6	18
22	1	1	2	2	4	1	1	2	5	2	5	1	4	1	1	4	4	2	3	6	18
23	5	1	2	1	2	1	1	1	5	2	4	1	4	5	1	4	3	2	3	6	18
24	5	1	2	1	1	1	2	5	4	2	2	1	2	5	2	2	3	2	3	6	18
25	5	1	2	1	2	3	2	1	2	2	3	5	1	3	2	1	3	1	3	6	18
26	5	1	2	2	2	4	2	5	1	1	3	2	2	5	1	3	3	2	3	6	18
27	2	3	2	2	1	5	3	1	1	2	1	2	2	2	5	1	1	1	3	6	18
28	1	2	5	4	1	4	3	1	1	5	1	3	3	2	4	1	1	1	3	4	12
29	1	2	5	2	1	4	3	1	2	5	1	4	2	2	5	1	1	1	3	4	12
30	5	2	1	2	2	1	2	5	2	3	3	1	3	5	1	3	3	1	1	10	10
31	1	2	1	5	1	2	5	1	1	3	1	2	4	1	1	2	5			5	10
32	1	1	2	2	5	1	1	2	5	3	5	1	4	1	1	3	4	2	2	4	8
33	5	1	2	1	2	3	2	5	2	2	1	1	4	2	3	2	1	1	1	8	8
34	1	2	5	3	1	3	3	2	3	5	1	4	3	2	5	2	2	1	2	4	8
35	1	2	2	2	4	1	1	2	5	2	4	1	4	1	1	3	4	2	1	6	6
36	1	1	2	2	5	1	1	1	5	2	5	1	4	1	1	4	4	2	3	2	6
37	1	1	3	2	4	1	1	1	3	5	1	5	1	1	5	4	2	1	6	6	
38	1	1	3	2	5	1	1	2	5	2	4	1	3	1	1	4	3	2	1	6	6
39	5	1	2	1	2	3	2	4	2	2	1	2	5	1	1	1	3	2	1	6	6
40	5	1	2	2	2	2	2	4	3	2	1	1	5	1	4	2	2	1	6	6	
41	5	1	2	2	2	2	2	4	3	2	1	1	1	5	1	4	2	1	1	6	6
42	5	1	2	3	2	2	2	5	2	2	3	1	2	5	1	4	3	2	1	6	6
43	5	2	2	2	2	4	2	5	2	2	3	1	3	5	1	5	3	2	1	6	6
44	5	1	2	1	1	3	2	5	2	2	3	1	3	5	1	3	3	2	1	6	6
45	5	1	2	2	2	1	2	4	2	3	2	3	5	1	3	2	1	6	6		
46	5	1	1	1	1	2	5	2	1	2	1	3	5	1	4	3	2	1	6	6	
47	5	1	2	2	3	2	5	2	2	2	3	5	1	2	2	1	6	6			
48	5	1	2	2	2	3	2	4	2	1	1	2	3	5	1	2	2	2	1	6	6
49	2	3	2	2	1	5	3	2	1	2	1	3	2	3	5	2	1	1	2	3	6
50	2	3	4	2	1	4	3	2	1	2	1	3	2	3	5	1	1	1	2	3	6
51	3	3	2	2	1	5	3	2	1	3	1	3	2	2	5	1	2	1	2	3	6
52	2	3	2	2	2	5	1	2	1	2	1	3	2	3	5	1	1	1	2	3	6
53	2	3	2	2	2	4	2	2	1	3	1	3	2	2	5	1	2	1	2	3	6
54	3	5	4	2	1	5	3	2	1	3	1	3	2	2	5	1	2	1	2	3	6
55	3	3	2	2	1	5	3	3	1	1	1	3	2	2	4	1	1	1	2	3	6
56	2	2	4	2	1	5	1	2	1	3	1	3	2	3	5	1	2	1	2	3	6
57	3	3	2	1	2	5	2	2	1	3	1	2	1	3	5	1	2	1	2	3	6
58	2	2	2	2	1	5	3	1	1	1	1	3	2	3	4	2	1	1	2	3	6

Note: AR1:BL58 defines the top right section of the survey data. (AR1 refers to the label for question 9, item 1, while BL58 refers to the profitability index score of respondent 57.)

Middle Right Section (AR59:BL115)

Row	AR	AS	AT	AU	AV	AW	AX	AY	AZ	BA	BB	BC	BD	BE	BF	BG	BH	BI	BJ Loc	BK Sea	BL Pro
59	1	2	5	3	1	3	3	1	1	5	1	4	2	2	5	2	2	1	1	4	4
60	1	2	1	5	1	4	5	3	1	2	1	5	3	1	2	4	2	1	1	4	4
61	1	2	1	4	1	4	5	1	1	2	1	5	3	1	2	5	2	1	1	4	4
62	5	2	1	2	1	3	2	5	2	2	2	2	3	5	2	3	2	2	1	3	3
63	5	1	1	3	2	1	2	5	3	3	1	1	3	4	2	3	3	2	1	3	3
64	5	2	1	3	1	1	2	5	2	3	2	1	3	4	1	5	3	2	1	3	3
65	5	1	2	1	2	3	2	5	2	1	2	1	3	5	1	3	3	2	1	3	3
66	5	1	1	2	2	2	2	5	3	1	2	2	4	5	1	5	2	1	1	3	3
67	5	1	1	3	1	3	2	5	2	2	2	1	3	5	2	1	3	2	1	3	3
68	5	1	2	2	2	2	2	5	1	3	2	2	2	5	1	3	3	2	1	3	3
69	5	1	2	3	2	4	2	2	2	2	1	3	4	1	4	2	1	1	1	3	3
70	5	1	1	3	1	1	2	5	2	2	2	1	3	5	1	3	2	2	1	3	3
71	5	1	2	3	2	3	2	5	1	2	2	1	3	5	2	5	3	2	1	3	3
72	5	2	2	3	1	3	2	5	2	3	2	1	3	5	1	4	3	2	1	3	3
73	5	1	1	2	2	3	2	5	2	2	3	1	1	5	1	3	3	2	1	3	3
74	5	2	2	1	2	3	2	5	2	2	1	1	1	5	1	5	3	1	1	3	3
75	5	1	1	3	1	2	2	5	1	2	2	1	3	5	2	3	3	2	1	3	3
76	5	1	2	3	2	3	2	5	2	2	2	1	3	4	1	3	2	1	1	3	3
77	5	1	2	2	2	3	2	5	2	2	2	1	3	5	2	3	3	2	1	3	3
78	3	4	4	1	2	5	2	2	1	1	1	2	1	2	4	2	2	1	1	3	3
79	3	3	2	2	1	5	1	2	1	2	1	3	2	2	5	1	2	1	1	3	3
80	2	5	1	1	1	5	3	2	1	1	1	2	1	3	5	1	1	1	1	3	3
81	3	3	4	2	1	5	3	3	1	2	1	2	1	2	5	2	1	1	1	3	3
82	2	3	2	1	1	5	2	2	1	2	1	2	1	3	5	2	1	1	1	3	3
83	1	3	5	2	1	3	3	1	2	5	1	3	3	2	5	2	1	1	1	2	2
84	2	3	5	2	1	4	2	1	2	5	1	4	2	2	4	1	2	1	1	2	2
85	1	1	5	2	2	4	2	1	2	5	1	5	3	2	5	1	2	1	1	2	2
86	1	2	1	5	1	2	5	1	1	2	1	5	3	2	2	3	2	1	1	2	2
87	1	2	1	5	1	2	5	3	1	2	1	5	3	1	2	4	2	1	1	2	2
88	1	2	2	5	1	2	5	3	1	3	1	5	3	2	4	2	1	1	1	2	2
89	2	3	4	2	1	5	3	2	1	2	1	3	2	2	5	1	1	1	1	2	2
90	1	2	3	1	4	1	1	3	5	3	5	1	4	1	1	4	3	2	0	10	0
91	1	1	2	11	5	2	1	3	5	3	5	1	4	1	1	4	4	2	0	6	0
92	1	1	4	2	5	2	1	3	5	4	5	1	5	1	1	3	4	2	0	12	0
93	1	1	2	1	5	1	1	3	5	2	5	1	4	1	1	4	4	2	0	6	0
94	5	1	2	1	1	3	2	5	2	2	2	1	3	5	1	4	2	1	0	6	0
95	5	1	2	1	1	3	2	5	2	2	2	1	3	4	2	3	3	2	0	3	0
96	5	2	2	2	2	2	5	3	1	2	2	3	2	5	2	5	2	2	0	3	0
97	5	1	2	3	2	1	2	5	3	2	2	3	4	2	3	3	2	0	3	0	0
98	1	2	5	2	1	3	2	1	2	5	1	4	3	2	5	2	2	1	0	4	0
99	1	2	5	4	1	3	2	1	2	5	1	4	3	2	5	2	2	1	0	2	0
100	1	2	4	1	2	4	2	2	1	1	4	4	3	2	5	2	2	1	0	4	0
101	2	2	5	3	1	4	2	1	3	5	1	4	3	2	4	1	2	1	0	4	0
102	1	1	5	2	1	4	2	1	2	5	1	4	3	2	5	2	2	1	0	4	0
103	1	2	5	2	2	4	2	1	2	5	1	4	4	2	5	1	3	1	0	2	0
104	1	1	4	2	1	4	2	1	2	5	1	5	2	2	5	2	3	1	0	2	0
105	1	2	5	2	1	4	2	1	2	5	1	4	3	2	5	1	2	1	0	4	0
106	1	1	5	2	1	3	3	2	2	4	1	4	2	2	5	1	2	1	0	4	0
107	2	2	4	2	2	4	2	1	2	5	1	4	3	2	5	1	2	1	0	2	0
108	1	2	5	3	1	4	2	1	3	5	1	4	2	2	5	1	2	1	0	2	0
109	1	1	5	2	1	4	2	1	1	5	1	4	3	2	5	1	2	1	0	4	0
110	1	2	5	4	1	4	2	2	2	5	1	4	3	2	5	2	2	1	0	4	0
111	1	2	5	2	2	3	4	1	2	5	1	5	3	2	5	1	3	1	0	4	0
112	1	2	4	3	1	4	2	1	2	4	1	5	3	2	5	1	2	1	0	2	0
113	1	2	5	2	1	4	2	2	2	5	1	3	3	2	5	1	2	1	0	4	0
114	1	1	5	2	1	4	2	1	2	5	1	4	3	2	5	1	1	1	0	4	0
115	1	2	5	2	1	4	2	1	2	5	1	4	3	2	5	1	2	1	0	2	0

Note: AR59:BL115 defines the middle right section of the survey data. (AR59 refers to question 9, item 1, as rated by respondent 58, while BL115 refers to the profitability index score of respondent 114.)

Bottom Right Section (AR116:BL170)

Rc	AR	AS	AT	AU	AV	AW	AX	AY	AZ	BA	BB	BC	BD	BE	BF	BG	BH	BI	BJ Log	BK Seat	BL Prof
116	1	2	5	3	2	2	2	1	2	5	1	5	3	2	5	1	2	1	0	4	0
117	1	1	5	2	1	4	2	1	2	4	1	4	3	2	4	1	2	1	0	4	0
118	2	2	5	2	1	4	2	1	2	5	1	4	4	2	5	3	2	1	0	2	0
119	1	2	5	2	1	3	2	1	1	5	1	4	2	2	5	1	2	1	0	4	0
120	1	3	4	2	1	4	4	1	2	5	1	4	3	2	5	1	2	1	0	4	0
121	1	2	5	4	1	4	2	1	2	5	1	4	3	2	5	1	1	1	0	4	0
122	1	2	5	2	1	4	2	1	2	5	1	4	3	2	5	1	2	1	0	4	0
123	1	2	1	5	1	2	5	1	1	2	1	5	2	1	2	5	2	1	0	2	0
124	1	2	1	4	1	3	5	1	1	2	1	5	3	2	1	5	2	1	0	2	0
125	2	2	2	5	1	2	5	2	1	3	1	5	2	1	2	4	1	1	0	2	0
126	1	3	1	5	1	4	5	1	1	2	1	5	3	1	1	5	2	1	0	4	0
127	1	2	1	4	1	2	4	1	1	2	1	5	3	1	2	3	2	1	0	2	0
128	1	2	1	5	1	3	5	2	1	4	1	5	3	1	2	5	2	1	0	5	0
129	1	3	1	5	1	2	5	1	1	2	1	5	2	2	1	5	3	1	0	2	0
130	1	2	2	4	1	2	5	1	1	3	1	5	3	1	2	5	2	1	0	2	0
131	1	2	1	5	1	4	5	2	1	2	1	5	3	1	2	5	1	1	0	4	0
132	1	2	1	5	1	2	5	1	1	3	1	5	3	1	2	4	2	1	0	2	0
133	1	2	1	5	1	2	4	1	1	3	1	5	3	2	2	5	1	1	0	4	0
134	2	2	1	5	1	3	5	1	1	2	1	5	3	1	2	5	2	1	0	5	0
135	1	2	1	4	1	2	5	2	1	2	1	5	3	1	1	4	2	1	0	2	0
136	1	3	1	5	1	2	5	1	1	5	1	5	2	1	2	5	1	1	0	4	0
137	1	2	1	5	1	4	5	3	1	2	1	5	3	1	2	5	2	1	0	4	0
138	1	2	2	5	1	2	4	2	1	2	1	5	3	1	1	5	3	1	0	5	0
139	1	2	1	4	1	4	5	1	1	4	1	5	2	1	2	5	2	1	0	2	0
140	1	2	1	5	1	2	5	1	1	2	1	5	3	1	2	4	2	1	0	2	0
141	1	2	1	5	1	2	5	1	1	2	1	5	3	1	1	5	2	1	0	4	0
142	1	2	1	5	1	3	5	2	1	2	1	5	3	1	2	5	2	1	0	2	0
143	1	2	2	4	1	2	4	1	1	2	1	5	2	2	2	5	2	1	0	4	0
144	1	3	1	5	1	4	5	3	1	2	1	5	3	1	1	5	2	1	0	7	0
145	2	2	1	5	1	2	5	1	1	3	1	5	2	1	2	5	1	1	0	5	0
146	1	3	1	5	1	2	5	1	1	2	1	5	2	1	1	5	2	1	0	5	0
147	2	3	4	2	1	5	3	1	1	3	1	3	2	4	5	1	1	1	0	3	0
148	2	3	2	2	1	4	2	2	1	3	1	3	2	3	5	1	1	1	0	3	0
149	2	4	1	1	2	5	2	2	1	1	1	2	1	4	4	1	1	1	0	3	0
150	3	4	4	2	1	5	3	1	1	1	1	3	1	4	5	1	1	1	0	3	0
151	2	3	2	2	1	4	3	2	1	2	1	3	2	4	5	1	1	1	0	3	0
152	9.1	9.2	9.3	9.4	9.5	10.1	10.2	10.3	10.4	10.5	11.1	11.2	11.3	11.4	11.5	12	13	14	Logal	Seats	Profit
153	150	150	150	150	150	150	150	150	150	150	150	150	150	150	150	150	150		150	150	150
154																		SUM	158	799	1285
155	2.21	1.82	2.54	2.63	1.99	2.83	2.5	2.36	2.25	2.75	2.01	2.75	2.86	2.43	2.6						

156								seats	count	seats		profit	count
157	Value Mean		Media Mean		Age	%	Incom	%	Gende	%	2	27	54	60	1
158	reedo	2.8	TY Come	2.9	Under 3	28%	Struggl	19%	Male	65%	3	39	117	54	9
159	Best	2.8	Pop. Mech	2.8	30s	10%	Strive	43%	Femal	35%	4	32	128	36	8
160	genui	2.5	Extreme S	2.6	40s	17%	Achiev	23%	Gende Other Target	5	5	25	24	1
161	Natur	2.4	Waterwa C	2.4	50s	24%	Vealth	15%	Male	73% 30%	6	23	138	18	7
162	Statu	2.3	Homes on F	2.0	60 or Ol	21%			Femal	27% 70%	7	1	7	12	2
163											8	1	8	10	2
164	Values Other set Market		Media Other set Market		Age Other set Market		Incom Other set Ma				10	2	20	8	3
165	Statu	1.8 4.0	Homes on F	1.5 3.9	Under 3	33% 10%	Struggl	20% 13%			12	10	120	6	24
166	Best	2.9 2.4	TY Come	2.7 3.6	30s	12% 3%	Strive	53% 3%			16	1	16	4	3
167	Natur	2.5 2.0	Waterwa C	2.6 1.8	40s	17% 17%	Achiev	21% 30%			18	9	162	3	21
168	reedo	3.1 1.7	Extreme S	2.9 1.4	50s	17% 53%	Vealth	6% 53%			20	1	20	2	7
169	genui	2.8 1.5	Pop. Mech	3.1 1.4	60 or ol	23% 17%					Sum	815		Sum	88
170	BINS	0	2	3	4	6	8	9	10	12	18	24	36	54	60

Note: AR116:BL170 defines the bottom right section of the survey data. (AR116 refers to question 9, item 1, as rated by respondent 115, while BL170 refers to the bottom right of the relevant analysis.)

Notes

Chapter 1

1. Luke 6:31: Today's New International Version of the Holy Bible (TNIV).

Chapter 3

1. Pareto (1984).
2. Pareto (1896/7).
3. Zipf (1949).
4. Newman (2005, January), p. 2.
5. Pareto (1984), p. 73.
6. Pareto (1984), p. 25.

Chapter 4

1. Zipf (1949), p. 39.
2. Juran (1951), pp. 38–39.
3. Koch (1998), p. 8–9.
4. Koch (1998), throughout.
5. Koch (2006), throughout.
6. Ferriss (2007), overall conclusion.

References

Churchill, G. A., & Brown, T. J. (2007). *Basic marketing research* (6th ed.). Mason, OH: Thomson South-Western.

Ferriss, T. (2011). *The 4-hour workweek: Escape 9–5, live anywhere, and join the new rich*. New York, NY: Random House.

Juran, J. M. (1951). *Quality control handbook*. New York, NY: McGraw-Hill.

Koch, R. (1998). *The 80/20 principle: The secret of achieving more with less*. New York, NY: Doubleday.

———. (2006). *The breakthrough of 16x: Real simple innovation for 16 times better results*. Dallas, TX: Pritchett.

Kotler, P., & Armstrong, G. (2010). *Principles of marketing* (13th ed.). Upper Saddle River, NJ: Prentice Hall.

Newman, M. E. J. (2005, January). Power laws, Pareto distributions, and Zipf's law. *Contemporary Physics 46*, 323–351.

Pareto, V. (1896/7). *Cours d'economie politique* [Course in political economy]. Lausanne, Switzerland: Rouge.

———. (1984). *Trasformazione della democrazia* [The transformation of democracy]. Milan, Italy: Corbaccio.

Zipf, G. K. (1949). *Human behavior and the principle of least effort*. Cambridge, MA: Addison Wesley.

Index

Announcing the Business Expert Press Digital Library

Concise E-books Business Students Need for
Courses and Research

This book can also be purchased in an e-book collection by your library as

- a one-time purchase,
- that is owned forever,
- allows for simultaneous readers,
- has no restrictions on printing,
- can be downloaded as PDFs from within the library community.

Our digital library collections are a great solution to beat the rising cost of textbooks. E-books can be loaded into their course management systems or onto students' E-book readers.

The **Business Expert Press** digital libraries are very affordable, with no obligation to buy in future years.

For more information, please visit **www.businessexpertpress.com/librarians**. To set up a trial in the United States, please contact **Sheri Allen** at *sheri.allen@globalpress.com*; for all other regions, contact **Nicole Lee** at *nicole.lee@igroupnet.com*.

OTHER TITLES IN OUR MARKETING STRATEGY COLLECTION

Collection Editor: **Naresh Malhotra**, *Nanyang Technological Institute, Singapore, and Georgia Institute of Technology, USA*

www.ingramcontent.com/pod-product-compliance
Lightning Source LLC
Chambersburg PA
CBHW062035200326
41519CB00017B/5046